A Practical Summary & Workbook for Using Jordan Peterson's "Maps of Meaning" to Sort Yourself Out

A Practical Summary & Workbook for Using Jordan Peterson's "Maps of Meaning" to Sort Yourself Out

Annette Poizner

Lobster University Press

Toronto, Canada

Contents

1

Introduction

In the front matter of Jordan Peterson's book, *Maps of Meaning: The Architecture of Belief*, you find a simple quotation: "I will utter things which have been kept secret from the foundation of the world. (Mathew 13:35). Indeed, Peterson's book relates to an aspect of life that is most central to our lives, yet mostly 'secret', invisible to us.

Based on your direct perceptions, your life experience, cultural and religious teachings you have integrated and learnings from science and other studies, you have formed a map. You use this map to interpret reality and move within it. This isn't an old dusty relic stored in the safety deposit box. This is the working map that guides you everyday and emboldens you with a sense that you have a reasonable grasp of reality, a good working model of truth and an informed sense of good and bad. You run your ship using this map. . . . and the map is invisible! You have only a hazy or partial sense of what is on it, where it is, how it formed. It's populated with beliefs, values and ideas you don't necessarily remember codifying. And, it turns out, your map may or may not serve your higher purposes. It definitely aims you somewhere; you may only be partially cognizant of where it aims and may or may not notice how it propels you in those very directions.

How strange when you think of it. This map, so foundational to who you are and how you function, is a veritable secret. People are in the dark about the full contents of their own personal map.

For the last 18 months, I've been busily taking notes from Peterson's book and lectures, especially from the first two chapters of *Maps of Meaning* which are most relevant to the tasks of psychotherapy. I'm presenting here a bite size chunk of the sorts of ideas that can, in my estimation, help you better understand yourself. My summary will be 'low resolution'; I'm focusing on the ideas that directly relate to the map of life that each person creates, to help you achieve greater levels of self-insight which you can then use to make tangible life changes.

As a psychotherapist, I can tell you that *Maps of Meaning* showcases ideas that are not currently mainstream in the clinical world. Your therapist may discuss your 'map of meaning', but not in this depth, with this slant. If you are looking for insight that can drive your self-awareness, the first part of this book is designed to take you on a tour of some of Peterson's ideas, and the second part of the book introduces a method that people can use to see the map of self and others, in relief. This technique, developed by Alfred Adler, one of the fathers of modern day psychology, is usually administered by trained therapists, but I've included it here because it provides a window into the map, a really interesting way we can see the map at play in the life of an individual.

Why Change the Map?

Every now and then, someone comes along and helps a generation of people become aware of the map of meaning, creating a consciousness that forever changes our ideas about ourselves and our psychology. Freud was one such figure. You may have read others. More recently, Peterson has triggered awareness, teaching university courses, speaking prolifically, writing his books. He has brought our attention back to the map and to the fact that we usually need to change the map, if we hope to change.

Changing that map is not easy. Changing behaviour is hard; changing the actual operating instructions . . . really hard! A killer! Yet, tackling that monumental task, cleaning the room *within*, is a gamechanger. If you do, you can achieve goals that seemed completely out of reach.

How can changing the map change your life? Grace (not her real name) described how Jordan Peterson's work helped her upgrade her map and change her life. In an email to me, she described the initial map she had been using, how it lead her off track, and the benefits she accrued when she explored Peterson's work:

> I followed the self-actualizing map for a long time, which is quite postmodern in its approach and I found that it doesn't work, in fact it took me into narcissistic territory and beyond that, nihilism. That map ended in the trip to the underworld as JP would say. At this point I burned my map completely – existential crisis of great magnitude. I will not expand on that but trust me, it was a doozy. After a period of groundlessness I have reoriented with JP's help.
>
> I have found the ease and joy of using a well-worn map while creating meaning and value in a life that includes both suffering and joy. I took myself out of the center of my map and inserted G-d. This is a major map changer. All my orienting questions shifted as I have gone from

> leader to follower. The experience I have now is that I didn't really make the map (what a relief) but I'm able to expand it, to be guided and it is a unique shared process with the Creator. When you realize you can follow a good map (an archetype such as Jesus) the journey just becomes so rich and meaningful. You are treading on the paths of great men and women which feels really supportive and exhilarating. JP is mapping out so much for us.
>
> I feel like I wandered in the desert like the Israelites and it was my own disobedience and insistence that I lead that made me go in circles for so long, lost to myself. There has to be an element of faith in my map of meaning. Without it, [life} is just a concept and not an embodied worthwhile experience. JP talks often about 'living as if there is a G-d' and having someone to 'bend your knee to' – without this element the map feels void of true value to me and life itself becomes futile.

For Grace, her new map seeded greater spirituality; others who have been influenced by Peterson's ideas became employable, more successful in family and intimate relationships, better disciplined, oriented to meaning versus fun (and consequently, less self-destructive). Read the comments below each YouTube video, thousands of testimonials left by fans who claim Peterson's teachings have changed their lives, creating a very different consciousness that helps them live better. Just a few examples:

> I feel as though I've been slapped in the face. I've spent so much time worrying about others around me, I've let dragons take over my life.
>
> I want you to know that your words and ideas have helped me become the father I need to be to break the chain of poverty, addiction and abuse that plagues my family tree so that my children can have a better life than I had. You have helped me find meaning in my life; to improve myself so that those who come after can have a better chance . . . You are more of a father to me than any other mortal man has ever been.

> Jordan Peterson, you're amazing... You've changed my life. If I could meet one person on this planet, it's YOU. I'd move heaven and earth for five minutes with you.
>
> I've never in my life bought a book. I've never had the interest. My book arrives in three days and I cannot wait to read it.
>
> My book marker for 12 rules is my empty antidepressant tablet case

On and on, the comments reveal a generation of people who are revising their map of meaning. It's exciting!

Why I Bothered

I first learned about Jordan Peterson from a psychotherapy client. This guy, a Peterson fan, made serious life changes. Peterson's ideas had been pivotal to his process. I was so impressed, I wanted to learn more about this renegade therapist. I listened, I read. The book, *Maps of Meaning*, was dense but I found content that was invaluable. It occurred to me that this content needed to be more accessible for people struggling to make changes in their lives.

In one year, 3 million copies of his bestselling book "12 Rules for Life" have been sold. That book is being translated into 50 languages. His lectures and videos have been watched by millions of people. There is bona fide wisdom in his approach. These days, though, postmodernism rules. Postmodernism views frames as social constructs, optional at best; there are no absolutes. Mindfulness meditation, which helps you drop frames and premises (and which is psychologically useful, for sure) is a good fit for the post-modernists. Cognitive Behavioral Therapy (CBT) is also a good modality for them. CBT helps people identify and change their thought patterns. These sorts of modalities fit the postmodernist frame nicely because the assumption here is that reality can be represented in many different ways. There is no one truth.

Peterson's ideas, in contrast, stand in sharp conflict. Peterson tells us that reality has contours that are absolute and can be defined. He asserts that if we acknowledge these aspects of reality and work with reality as it is, we will be more effective, psychologically healthier and live more meaningful lives. He asserts that those truths are implicitly depicted and relayed in myths and classic stories; that we implicitly learn about the nature of reality by reading these works, particularly at a young age. If he's right, if reality has characteristics that we can define and know in some absolute sense, then there would be rules, best practices, for living productively within that reality. Peterson articulates these rules. Postmodernists vehemently disagree.

Given all this, I came to the conclusion that certain ideas described at length in *Maps of Meaning* need to be more accessible. Peterson's insights can help people understand their map, a map which leads them to their best destiny . . . or not. Given how important it can be for people to access this look into their own guiding 'software', I humbly decided to take on this project. Humbly, because this is a living document. I will keep updating this book as I find ways to add or improve, always in the spirit of better representing Peterson's work.

Keeping it Simple . . . and Practical

In Peterson's book, he gives us a behind the scenes look at what we do know about the contours of reality. He examines how our own circuitry, the neuropsychology of the brain, influences how we represent reality to ourselves. He looks at mythology around the world which depicts patterns of reality in a veiled way and implicitly departs lessons how to live within reality. The various cultures create myths and narratives to seed shared maps/understandings amongst the members of society so as to promote harmony and good citizenship in that society. Peterson slides back the curtain and helps make us conscious of the various forces and influences that shape the map of meaning. He helps create more awareness about how we depict reality to ourselves and how we architect a path forward using the map of our own making. And he covers a lot more. But my focus is very narrow.

For me, the important concepts in this book which relate to the change process are the following:

- the concept of the map of meaning, an implicit map of reality which guides each individual forward, usually out of conscious awareness.
- hallmarks of a healthy and productive map of meaning. The most productive map is one in which the individual identifies with the archetype of the hero, reflecting a commitment to a fundamentally active approach (versus, worse case scenario, subscribing to a victim mentality).
- the various permutations that we find in peoples' maps. One map orients the person towards nihilism, another pitches the individual towards a rigid ideology (as Peterson says, quoting Jung, "ideas have people"); in both of these just-mentioned cases, the individual has failed to cultivate a useful map of life.
- the fact that the optimal map is one that accurately represents reality and, as a consequence, the individual achieves better outcomes.

- a description by Peterson of his understanding of reality and its' contours.
- the argument that people must update their maps, especially when it becomes clear that they have been harbouring misunderstandings about reality. [1].
- the idea that certain formulations of reality have taken root in popular culture, conceptualizations which directly contradict the nature of reality (as Peterson understands it). Each time an erroneous idea takes hold of a person, that person is more likely to veer off-track, falling into unproductive habits or negative outcomes.

In this work, I am explaining and summarizing the above-mentioned core ideas so that readers can learn about the map of meaning which helps each person navigate a reality that is often ambiguous and confusing. I want to strip down Peterson's work and simplify those ideas which can help you sort yourself out and move your life 'out of chaos to habitable order', to quote Peterson.

In the following chapters I am summarizing what I believe is the most therapeutically useful material found in Peterson's text, and hope that it helps readers 'sort themselves out!' If you are primarily looking for a synopsis of Peterson's thoughts and premises in his *Maps of Meaning* book, you may be done reading after the first 4 chapters. My hope would be that by providing a concise summary of this sort, would serve as a roadmap you could use to make life changes and better operationalize Peterson's teachings.

Additionally, though, I am including several chapters which summarize relevant ideas of an important theorist, Alfred Adler. Adler developed a method for analyzing early memories to garner insight into the personal map of meaning of any given individual. This technique is practiced by Adlerian therapists and there are seasoned practitioners in major city centers around the world who use it. I'm introducing this Adlerian technique because it gives us an interesting way to see the map of meaning rendered quite explicitly. Additionally, readers might be able to use the technique to access their map of meaning, either working independently or in conjunction with a therapist. The Adlerian insights have much to bring to the discussion of the map of meaning and, therefore, the second part of this book showcases these ideas and is there for readers who are curious to learn more about it.

Who are You?

You may love listening to Peterson and reading his books. You may read and listen and wished you comprehended more of it. Maybe you find some of his ideas intriguing while you strongly disagree with others. Maybe you can't stand him, but it wouldn't hurt to figure out what his core thesis so you can tear it down. Whoever you are, if the idea of seeing Peterson's basic worldview stated briefly sounds helpful, this book may be a good learning aid for you.

More specifically, I've written this piece with several readers in mind:

The Curious. You may be somebody who has wondered what all the fuss is about. Maybe you listened to Peterson but found his ideas elusive owing to his academic style or to the many tangents that he takes. For you, my goal has been to articulate central tenets of his thesis in an organized way. If I have succeeded, you may find that reading the next four chapters lets you pick up *Maps of Meaning: The Architecture of Belief* and better understand it.

The Critic. If you are the person who's been triggered by Peterson's 'politics' but still find yourself curious about aspects of his work that seem to be resonating with people, I believe my summary captures ideas that speak to the question of how people might productively live their lives.

The Fan. Maybe you are a Jordan Peterson enthusiast, the type who wants to keep up with anything Peterson, I'd like to introduce you to some other theorists you will probably like and also advance a technique you might find intriguing.

The Challenged. You may be somebody going through personal challenges. You've heard of Peterson and understand that many have found his ideas helpful. You'd like to see if there's something there that can help you out, but you may not be willing to wade through long analyses of world myths. I'd like to think that I've summarized important ideas that will help you understand yourself and your current dilemma.

The Practical. As I have said, Peterson often presents ideas in a circuitous way. You go for a ride; you learn about the myth, you learn about the brain. Some people like to go everywhere he goes; others may have an appetite to focus exclusively on the psychology without extraneous learnings that can make the core principles harder to access. I'm definitely writing this for you, and I'm actually that type of person myself. I offer this book, extremely grateful to Peterson who has so generously shared his opus of work.

On a Practical Note...

In this book, sometimes I will be quoting Peterson directly, other times paraphrasing. When I do quote, I draw from notes I have made in the course of listening to countless lectures over the course of months. I am not footnoting the specific lecture from which any given quote is drawn. With no thought or plan to write about his work, I did not keep detailed records! So I apologize for that lack of specificity. Just know that when I quote him, the phrase was his!

In the next chapter, we will start where Peterson himself starts, looking at a fundamental question: What is reality? The absolute structure of reality will determine how we process reality. We will then see how each person cultivates a map of meaning to help them with the task of living in a world where the landscape of reality is often times ambiguous and chaotic.

Notes

1. Alfred Adler asserted that "faulty evaluation is at the root of all mental disease." Peterson would agree with that statement.

Part 1

2

Jordan Peterson on 'Reality'

What is reality?

Peterson suggests that your basic premises about reality, likely influenced by the way that science has advanced our lives, may be wrong.

Based on what you see, you might conclude that ours is a world of things. Objects are comprised of atoms or molecules. Cells are the constituent part of people and animals. Sound breaks down into sound waves and so on. So we think, as per the discoveries of science, that our world is, first and foremost, physical. In fact, our worldview is so influenced by science that the idea is pervasive: things are the stuff of life. Ours is a world of things.

Not so fast. Peterson points out that, despite our first impressions, we live in a world of value. Whenever we see some facet of the physical world, what 'is' exists alongside 'what could be'.

If you're an interior designer, you walk into a room and note the decoration but in your mind's eye you quickly come up with your vision of a better layout, furniture that would be better in this space. The judge who watches the Olympic athlete sees the athletic performance and compares it in the minds' eye to what the most ideal performance would look like. That internally generated standard will determine whether the athlete gets a medal and, if so, which medal. A seasoned cook tastes the food and, comparing the taste to the standard that exists in the 'inner palette', knows which spices to add.

Similarly, the same dichotomy exists in how you experience your own life. In any moment, you have a current reality and you have goals. If you're in university, you are sitting in a classroom taking notes, but you are directed to your meta-outcome: graduating and getting a good job. You don't live in the present moment with the conception of yourself and your life as perfect as is. You have a number of goals you are working towards. Hopefully you retain those goals at the front of your mind at all times. So you live in the present and in the future, simultaneously.

If the current state of anything is incomplete without a vision of what it could become, then the real nature of the world is action; a series of actions will be required to bring anyone/anything to an improved state. And science can't help us figure out the exact actions that will help any given person move forward, given his or her unique situation. Science helps us understand the objective world, but it deliberately removes the subjective element. Yet, it is the subjective element that we must mull over to come up with the unique life path for each of us.

According to Peterson, to the degree that individuals cobble together a useful map for themselves, aiming themselves towards appropriate outcomes and taking reasonable actions to move forward, is the degree to which they will experience meaning in life. To the degree that individuals' maps are poorly conceived and aim them badly, they flounder, feel depressed and are prone to negativity. After all, daily life is peppered with bad news, tragedy, illness. If there is no vision of productive action which could improve things, the present is unchanging; hopeless. At worse, people become nihilistic, negative about life itself.

As Peterson says, "you need a path that justifies the tragedy of life." The right motivation allows you to strive, to force forward in a way that suits you, allowing you to undertake well chosen behaviours designed to improve things, irregardless of challenges. A lot is going to ride on whether the map of life of any given individual serves the person or is somehow flawed and problematic. Clearly each person should take stock of his or her own map of life, even though it is implicit and not always easy to access. Peterson is introducing this priority to a generation of young people, and, in so doing, helping them change and upgrade outdated old maps that date back to childhood.

"We'll preserve for our children this, the last best hope of man on earth,
or we'll sentence them to take the last step into a thousand years of darkness."
Abraham Lincoln

So, to summarize, the elementary grammar of this world is the verb, not the noun. Ours is, first and foremost, a world of action which means that in any moment we need to figure out what to do to move life forward. We each, therefore, come up with a life map to guide the way and answer the myriad of questions that arise about how to move forward. What's the next step? How do I improve my life? Do I do what feels right or what sounds right? Right according to who? There are infinite visions, so many ways I can move. How do I figure out which way achieves the best outcome? My map will be a composite of all the answers that I generate in response to these, and other, questions.

The Known and the Unknown

Peterson adds another complexity that makes the task of living yet more confusing. There are two aspects to the world. There is the known world and the unknown world. Imagine a baby is born. Initially, the world itself, the crib, the nursery, the other children in the family and even the parents, exist as a mass of confusion for a baby that can't interpret the blur of sound, feeling and image. The baby is born into a world full of lights, sounds, stimuli – it's chaos! That baby is ill-equipped to detect and interpret all the patterns embedded in this complex landscape.

As the brain and body of the baby is gradually able to read patterns and otherwise begin mapping out reality, mother's face becomes familiar. That face corresponds, say, to positive outcomes. Baby smiles when she sees that face. Gradually the map expands. Other facets of that murky, confusing world become intelligible. This is brother. This is sister. More associations. As a child learns to talk, to write, aspects of the unknown world become known. Those letters that used to look like unintelligible black shapes now are discerned as parts of words. Those markings make sense now. For the child, life has moved from an experience of chaos to one of order.

When years later she takes algebra, at the beginning of that course, she knows how to read, but all those letters and formulas look like a mash of nonsense. By the end of the course, they will make sense. Another aspect of the world, formerly unknown, is now part of the universe she knows and understands. Every time an aspect of the unexplored territory is processed successfully, we get more rules, more wisdom, more distinctions, we advance our map. We benefit from so doing. We experience more mastery and are rewarded with feelings of stability and self-confidence.

Initially the unexplored domain is chaos and confusion. Later, once explored, we grasp the intrinsic order that initially eluded us. "Oh. Now I get it." It turns out that chaos usually has a potential for order that we can extract or create. We do so and now we've learned a few things. Our map is now more sophisticated; we can do more, move forward in ways we earlier could not.

As that process unfolds, as we move further afield and explore the unknown, we are undertaking the hero's journey. In Genesis, 12, 1, the text reads, "G-d said to Abram, 'Go for yourself from your land, from your relatives, and from your father's house to the land I will show you.' This command sanctions moving away from the familiar into the unknown, for all humanity, forevermore. We walk in Abraham's footsteps with each step forward, providing, of course, the movement is in a sanctioned direction ("the land I will show you") and not a stroll in no man's land! Premised here is the necessity of a relationship with the G-d ideal, something Peterson points out is lacking in secular society, but that will be discussed in an upcoming chapter.

So – to review – we are constantly meant to thrust forward. At any given time there are aspects of the world which we completely understand and other aspects that are a complete mystery and our task is to continue to approach and discover new terrain. As a kid, you learn to ride a bike. At age 16, it might be time for driving lessons. Bike riding has become old hat, as the saying goes, but the rules of the road as a driver of a car – that's unexplored territory – until you master it. You take your lessons, get some practice. That formerly unexplored territory is now explored. The next challenge awaits you, around the corner. And so on, and so forth.

Lest we assume that the unexplored dimension only relates to that which is outside of us, bear in mind that even our own bodies can trip us into an experience of the unexplored. Perhaps a person becomes sick and their body does not work as it did. These changes throw us into confusion and chaos. Even the removal of a tooth, Peterson reflects, will have us excavating the interior of the mouth with the tongue, potentially for months, as we recalibrate to the mouth that has become unfamiliar given the change of the interior landscape. Eventually the new circumstance becomes the new normal. We move from unknown to known, chaos to order.

And this is life. There is an infinite domain of realities, experiences, disciplines, etc.. The older we get, the more learnings and experience we accrue, the realm of the explored expands, the realm of the unexplored shrinks, the map gets more detailed and sophisticated; hopefully this process continues to our very last day, enhancing our competence, generating yet more wisdom. Still, some aspects of the unexplored territory will always remain unexplored. How can we understand some of the enigmas and paradoxes that science reveals but cannot explain? What happens after death? Is there a spiritual infrastructure to this world, something that we cannot see? Ultimately the unexplored territory takes us to the heart of mystery.

The 'Unknown Unknown'

Once we understand the concept of the unknown, Peterson introduces an additional concept: the "unknown unknown." Say you have a plan to study radiography. You begin your studies and while the topic has you dabbling in unknown territory, you have undertaken this study voluntarily and the process of learning is orderly. You are navigating the 'known unknown' towards the end of extending the dimension of reality you know to include radiography.

In sharp contrast, there are times we are hurtled into 'unknown territory' under duress, forced by unforeseen circumstances that occur suddenly. We call these events disasters or emergencies; also, the proverbial dark night of the soul. Whether it be a medical diagnosis, falling victim to a crime or accident or being betrayed by someone we thought we knew, the individual descends into chaos. The individual's world becomes foreign and unfamiliar. All bearings are lost. There is a greater level of strain associated with the "unknown unknown," potentially resulting in post-traumatic stress or a general depletion of resources (physical, emotional, financial, etc). The possibility of experiencing the 'unknown unknown' is always near at hand, a source of anxiety for the timid. Fearing unforeseen negative outcomes, some may defensively avoid the unknown dimension at all costs. Peterson also points out that because we can imagine our own death that fear can contaminate the realm of the unknown. "What if dabbling with the unexplored leads to death?" This fear conjures up additional worries regarding the unknown.

Life involves taking action and there are so many good reasons for feeling unsure about how to move forward. The physical world provides context but fails to provide clear directions. You see a given physical reality and you may be uncertain: how to birth what 'is' into a better outcome? And which outcome to pursue? Then: how to achieve the goal? How to make a new friend? How to resolve a health problem? Every day involves countless choices. What to eat? How to cook it? And considering your next move, there may be associated risks – the "unknown unknown" lurks in the background. What if you don't have all the information you need to prevent a misstep? So much of the terrain is unexplored. You could take a decisive action and face negative consequences you did not foresee.

Fortunately, we are outfitted with two parts of the brain, each of which is specialized to deal with one or the other aspect of reality, the known or the unknown. Together, we use them to cobble together a map of life, a task that we start in childhood, but continue doing throughout our lives. The right and left hemispheres are the tools we bring to the task of decoding reality; they allow us to face the unknown and build the map of meaning.

Right and Left Brain

Peterson talks extensively about how the two hemispheres work in tandem to help us orient to reality. He cites the work of Neuroscientist Elkhonon Goldberg who posits that the right brain and the left brain have specific roles to play, relative to the known and unknown dimensions of reality. The right brain orients to the realm of novelty, the unknown dimension. It takes a quick look at new situations/environments, surveying for patterns that are familiar. It's as if we take a picture of the big picture to see if any part reminds us of some other context that we have experienced or mastered.

You hear a sudden loud noise. You freeze. You scan the environment. Then, wordlessly you get your bearings, drawing upon past life experience which provides the only frame of reference you could possibly have. Finally the nonverbal right brain comprehends what's happening, where this noise came from and what it means. Next the left brain gears up, and puts words to the right brain's hunch. Using logic and analysis, the left brain provides a detailed sequence of directions or thoughts, allowing you to respond to your situation. "Close the window." "Call the police."

Let's say that you're in the kitchen doing a few simple kitchen chores. Suddenly, you notice sharp stinging pain in your eyes. You freeze in a state of vigilant awareness. You experience a pang of anxiety. That's the right brain's response when adjusting to novel circumstances. The negativity alerts you to stop everything and survey the situation. The right brain, faced with a sudden anomaly, surveys the scene, trying to detect a pattern. Memory flashes. The left brain then verbalizes what the right brain came up with: "oh, right. Cutting onions irritates the eyes!" Right brain has silently surveyed the context, searching for and finding stored learnings which generate the insight: "No emergency! This is a familiar pattern!" Now left brain articulates what's going on and triggers the details, thoughts about what I can do about this: "Turn on the kitchen fan." "Leave the room."

To summarize: the right brain registers negative affect, triggers a shut down of action and moves into a mode of vigilant observation. It perceives the *gestalt* of a situation, looking, metaphorically speaking, with a flood light at the big picture. It strives to clarify a situation or context, then hands the insight to the left brain which can put words to it. The left brain, the filing cabinet, stores details about any given aspect of reality. "How to cook vegetable soup? Here are the steps."

So we have these two parts of the mind, each of which specializes in helping us process either the known or unknown dimensions of reality. It is more comfortable dealing with the known dimension, of course. There is more predictability dealing with the known. The unknown, at least initially, may induce confusion, frustration or even overwhelm. But it also awakens our curiosity and facilitates mastery when we ultimately comprehend and manage that which initially confounded us.

Peterson suggests the healthiest, most stable, most satisfied individuals, those who find greatest meaning in life, are those "who live on the edge of what they know;" anchored in the zone of the familiar which provides stability, but dabbling with that which is new and unfamiliar, and subsequently energized by new thoughts and experiences. For Peterson, the person who rightly traverses the known and unknown dimensions of reality in a balanced way recreates paradise on earth "so that the forces of the cosmos are properly balanced in one's being and all feels right in the world."

The Stick in the Mud

Some people, though, insist on sticking with the familiar, avoiding the unexplored realm. "I just want to rely on what I know and leave it at that!" Bad plan. For one thing, there will be mental health ramifications. It could look like obsessive-compulsive disorder; somebody who overly fixates on the details and fails to activate the holistic pattern detecting right brain. The result is rigidity. A lack of wisdom. A person prone to repetition in thought and speech; the type who others experience as 'boring' and 'repetitive'; Someone who fixates on minutia; Someone necessarily prone to anxiety, further fuelling the drive to avoid anything unfamiliar.

Such a person quickly falls behind the times. Peterson gives the example of electronics which constantly need to be updated as current operating software becomes out of date. Peterson cites Alice in Wonderland; the Red Queen tells Alice, "in my kingdom, you have to run as fast as you can to stay in place." For Peterson, that quote represents the need to access aspects of the unknown just to keep up with everyone and everything else. After all, there are always new processes, new technologies, new visions, new mentalities coming down the pike. Keep your head in the sand and you become irrelevant. No wonder we tell seniors to learn a new language or take up a new sport. Dabbling with the unfamiliar keeps us fresh, vital, interested and interesting. Otherwise we stagnate.

"Wonder, not doubt, is the beginning of knowledge."
A. J. Heschel

The truth is even if you firmly resolved to only engage with that which you know, it wouldn't work. Anytime you try to achieve something, if it works the way you thought it would, you are in known territory. You get it. You achieved the outcome you were trying for, are satisfied, and ready to move on to your next goal. The problem is any number of times in life you try to achieve a particular outcome using the best of what you know to achieve success and. . . Damn! It didn't work!

Turns out your map was slightly off, given some variable you hadn't accommodated. You have hit a wall, entered the zone of the unknown. "Why didn't that work?" Using the right brain, you have to redouble your efforts and revisit what is now clearly unexplored terrain to figure out what you did wrong and how to get it right. You are like the GPS – "recalibrating, recalibrating."

Hopefully you figure it out, modify your behaviour and get your desired result. If you do, you have extended the explored terrain. Moving forward you will make more distinctions, ones you weren't aware of before, when navigating the same territory. You will feel more competent, experience a greater sense of security and stability.

So clearly even if you intend on never dabbling with the unknown, it's still going to find you! Wrestle with it, crack it open and pull out the understandings that had eluded you and you will grow. Walk away discouraged and resentful and you may become chronically bitter. More on that later.

This is the stuff of life. Or the way Peterson puts it: when we engage with the unknown we gather more information and in so doing we get further "formed." He says 'InFORMation' helps us to form ourselves! We don't just retool, we literally "reconstitute" ourselves. In other words, contact with the unknown strengthens and builds our core identities. It changes who we are. And every day provides more opportunity to reach into another bit of unknown territory and thereby expand our map . . . and ourselves.

The Resistant Among Us

The more advantageous posture, we said, is to dabble with the unknown, in bite size increments. If some avoid the realm of the unexplored territory, others take it a step further. Consider a person who assumes a posture of certainty, the confident type who effectively asserts: "Everything I know is what I need to know. I don't need to know anything beyond that." Peterson characterizes this posture as pathological stultification. This individual is unwilling to explore new vistas.

In Peterson's mind, this person has made an alliance with the devil. They will prioritize their own personal interest. Peterson says their lives are a living hell. They will have a low tolerance for anything out of the ordinary and will react with heightened aggression when confronted with anything that challenges their vision, their politic, their status quo. They will be prone to paranoia, fixated on maintaining security (control) and seeing threat everywhere.

Why can they trust no one; not even life itself? People who can trust their own ability to delve into unknown territory experience resilience. They perceive themselves as strong and able. These people trust themselves and thus they can trust others and even life, itself. People who recoil from the unknown feel vulnerable and suspicious. They cannot trust.

The Map You Need

It becomes clear that not only do we need a map that will help us navigate both the unexplored and the explored terrain but, ideally, we need a map that strongly encourages us to explore both of these terrains, and each in the right way, at the right and appropriate moment. Avoiding the unexplored leads to rigidity but pursuing that domain excessively or prematurely can be detrimental, as well. Maybe a young person who delves into new areas – sexual experience, religious observance, esoteric knowledge – without adequate grounding, maturity or readiness, may find any of these realms to be over-stimulating and disorganizing. Too much of the unexplored terrain experienced too early or too intensely, wreaks havoc. Perhaps that's why we have the expression, "when the student is ready, the teacher appears." That saying could express a hope more than a fact!

As we go along, we realize that we need to move forward in deliberate measured ways, we must cultivate a map which will guide our efforts for the duration of a lifetime, and, since we don't come with operating instructions, putting together an accurate map is going to be a DIY project.

Culture to the Rescue!

Society is comprised of people, each of whom has to navigate a reality full of ambiguity – not only because of the unexplored territory. Ambiguity is also a product of life being dynamic. There are many changing circumstances to navigate in any given day. Each individual has different talents and weaknesses and he or she will need to manage and express them while also competently getting along with others and juggling different roles and circumstances. Each person must express and also regulate the self, while navigating whatever comes up. A good map will be key and that map better be available to us starting at a young age.

Damn. It's not.

So culture helps us out. Firstly, culture establishes a social order, creating norms and structures that help people live together in an organized way. Culture, therefore, advances its own map which guides interactions between people and establishes norms about how to relate in different contexts. True, these structures, implemented excessively can become tyrannical and oppressive. Despite that risk, the benefits have members of society living in harmony with each other. When citizens abide by the cultural norms and rules, they experience stability and avoid lives characterized by chaos and uncertainty.

Secondly, culture embeds specific knowledge, teaching implicit lessons that can help children understand the world while accessing ancestral wisdom that has accumulated over the generations. All this wisdom can be relayed in myth, in the language of the arts, in nursery rhymes.

Why through these mediums? We have already learned that the right brain is the portal of entry for learning about the unexplored dimension. If you wish to introduce new ideas, and if you want those ideas to stick, you best introduce them using the medium that specifically targets the right brain. The right brain activates with metaphor and story, imagination and emotion. The right brain processes myths and fables. Peterson frequently deconstructs iconic myths and stories, showing the embedded lessons that are relayed in the story and in the symbols within, hidden meanings which are lapped up by the right brain of the young child. Peterson demonstrates, in his fascinating writings and lectures, how society uses culture to help young people cultivate a working map that will help them learn how to live well amongst others and otherwise how to conduct themselves.

"Genuine poetry can communicate before it is understood."
T.S. Eliot

Let's look at one simple example that I draw from my frame of reference. Remember the children's story, *Little Red Riding Hood*? This little girl dressed in a red cape wanders through the forest to visit her grandmother. When she finally gets to grandmother's house she sees that Granny's facial patterns resemble those of a wolf. Indeed, the wolf has dressed in Granny's clothing.

Little Red Riding Hood undertakes a process. She doesn't just throw herself into interaction with Granny. She pauses, experiencing the hesitation typical of the right brain in the face of novel stimuli. Then she undergoes the pattern detection process associated with the right brain. Compare: Granny's eyes to these eyes. Granny's ears to these ears. Hmmm. In the end, the little girl correctly identifies that this is not her grandmother, first by activating her right brain, then, her left brain.

On first glance, we see a story that teaches the child that situations exist in which the normal explored terrain, visiting Granny, gives way, unexpectedly, to unexplored terrain. The story provides a lesson how the child can manage anomalous events, many of which will likely occur over the span of the child's lifetime. The story teaches children how to engage the right brain process of pattern detection to understand and manage unfamiliar situations. But is there more embedded in this tale?

Now if we deconstruct the message, think about the following. The color red associates, say, with the stop sign or a red traffic light. Stop! Sometimes red is an indicator of danger. According to one source, the wolf is a symbol representing the threat of rape.[1]

Interesting. Now we have a story that cloaks a little girl in red, the color that warns of danger. And while she's intending to meet her Granny, someone vitally concerned for her well being, she discerns that she is dealing with a predator, all this by doing a right brain analysis of the anomaly.

Could this be a metaphor? She properly identifies the wolf because she has cloaked herself in the red cape, representing a cautious outlook which trips her into the analysis that gets her to the right answer. We see a message embedded by culture for little girls who, many years later, will be navigating the world of boys! The culture quietly seeds the knowledge that there may be wolves who otherwise assume the guise of Granny. And culture communicates this teaching in a way that will not be detected by the child's conscious mind. How's that for implicit learning?

So many times, parents, culture has your back. Classic literature, fairytales, creative productions that have attracted widespread interest, often are carriers of important cultural messages. If Humpty Dumpty is so pervasive that it's known by three-year-olds as well as 90-year-olds, expect to find an important message embedded within it! Having said that, we also need to point out that any number of times there can be cultural productions which embed counterproductive teachings. An upcoming chapter addresses this. The point here is not to imply that every cultural message is productive. It is good to know, though, that some classic narratives communicate implicit truths given that each person has to come up with their own map of meaning and we can use whatever help we can access, in order to do so.

Chapter Summary

Though we may perceive reality as a world of things, Peterson points out that we actually live in a world of value. Whenever we see something in its current state, it exists, in our mind's eye, alongside what could be; we spend our lives working to achieve those higher visions. People don't live their lives striving to maintain their current circumstances. They strive to achieve goals they harbour which will improve and advance their lives. Therefore, the world is not a world of things; the world is a forum for action. Each individual must come up with his or her own path, deciding which actions to execute to achieve whatever outcomes deemed worthwhile.

Determining what actions to take is complicated because reality has two constituent parts: the known reality and the unknown aspect of reality. The unknown is so unfamiliar, we experience it as pure chaos. On one hand, we have to choose a course of action so as to create a meaningful future but on the other hand, we have to manage uncertainty given that many pockets of reality are unfamiliar; we have no clue how to traverse them. It becomes necessary for each person to cultivate a map. That map – hopefully – directs the individual to act in ways that will gradually expand the person's competence and confidence in dealing with that which is foreign.

Peterson points out that we each harbour this map, a fixture in the subconscious; we are not necessarily conscious that we have it. The map points us in certain directions, identifying desirable goals and identifying strategies that the person can use to achieve those goals.

When the landscape is known/familiar, the individual moves comfortably within it and has mapped out strategies for functioning. Known aspects of life are predictable and easy to navigate.

The unknown dimension is completely unfamiliar. The individual traverses it bit by bit and so gradually gains familiarity; ultimately that which was unknown becomes known. When this occurs, the individual has expanded the map. A part of what was the broader landscape, formerly disorienting, is now comfortable to inhabit. Peterson asserts that life requires us to master the unknown, bit by bit, over the course of life, literally until the day of death. There always will be aspects of the unknown to unpack and doing so imparts wisdom, confidence, competence and garners a sense of stability.

To the degree that a person extends into unknown territory and cultivates a working knowledge of it, is the extent to which the person cultivates a better and more detailed map of reality. The better the map, the more accurately it represents the territory, the more meaning a person experiences in life.

Peterson discusses the two hemispheres of the brain, each which specialize in a different type of function. The right hemisphere, nonverbal, has pattern detection skills which we can use when confronting the unknown dimension. This faculty lets us look globally at the situation to see if any part of it is familiar. If we can orient and find the familiar in the unknown, the left brain can then parse the details, coming up with a detailed response plan. The left brain has at its access an index of detailed strategies for acting in the realm of the known, amassed over time. In this way, we are equipped with what we need to tackle parts of reality that are unknown and potentially scary.

If we constantly access and struggle with aspects of the unknown territory we are constantly stimulated, challenged and growing. Yet there are people who resist and in so doing become rigid, prone to anxiety, obsessive and, worst case scenario, fall into an extreme state characterized by nihilism, negativity and a resistance to learn anything new.

This chapter focuses on how and why people cultivate a 'map of meaning', the map they use to interpret reality and decide how to act in the world. We see the importance of the map, especially given that aspects of the world are mysterious and unknown. Children, not cognitively mature, are charged with the task of making a map at an age/stage of development when they are ill-equipped to do so. Society helps the task via culture. Culture teaches learnings both by imposing norms but also embedding lessons within fables and narratives that speak directly to the right brain of the growing child. Culture therefore seeds values that help socialize children, teaching cooperative behaviour and role modeling appropriate ways to act.

Reflection Points

Consider journaling your answers to the following questions in order to make this content more immediately relevant to your life:

If reality is a world of action, what actions can you identify in your life that have moved you into meaningful territory?

In your life, which motivation/agenda energizes you and gives you strength to cope with aspects of your life that are negative, challenging and seem hard to change?

For you, what is the known world? What is in your domain of competence?

For you, what is in the domain of the unknown? Which areas of life are you still needing to master?

Are you tackling something unknown/chaotic in the landscape of your life right now? If there's something that you need to address can you break it down into small manageable steps? What would that look like? What benefits would doing so bring to your life?

Do you know people who resist dabbling with the unknown? Who? What are they like?

Notes

1. Rabbi Yitzchak Ginsburgh has discussed this in his writings

3

You Have a Map of Meaning

Starting at a very young age, a child begins to assemble a working map of reality. One of the fathers of modern-day psychology, Alfred Adler, discussed the way people cultivate this map over time. He came up with a term for the map, calling it 'life style'. I haven't heard Peterson discuss Adler's concept of lifestyle, but it's worth mentioning.

For Adlerians, the life style of the individual refers to that individual's unique, consistent pattern of thinking, feeling, and acting. The life style is the person's 'organizing principle' or "rule of rules," as if each individual harbours a 'blueprint' which dictates consistent ways of coping or behaving (Shulman & Mosak, 1988, p. 3). In other words, the life style is the map each person uses to interpret reality and determine ways of acting or responding.

How is this life style assembled over time? The learning of a child occurs in a process of trial and error. The small child assesses reality, moment by moment, and gradually abstracts rules to live by. At first, say Shulman & Mosak, any given rule is treated like a hunch. With time, if the rule seems to work, it is elevated to the status of law. Those laws harden into full-fledged beliefs with staying power. At that point, the child, so convinced of the veracity of the law, will be drawn to perceive the world through the lens of his or her belief. He will find more and more validation of the law; certainty sets in. So the point here: the law is reinforced because a person perceives only that which supports his or her prevailing beliefs. As Einstein said, "Believing is seeing."

Say your map tells you that people are not to be trusted. You will be riveted each and every time people disappoint you and will fail to register times people are reliable and warrant trust. If your map tells you everybody in your midst cannot be trusted, you, too, will become untrustworthy ("why should I be reliable when they are not?"). The map dictates what you see, what you do, and ultimately shapes your life! This is why Peterson says it is so important to examine that map. Initially the map helps us to orient ourselves and generate generalizations about life so we can make predictions about what will happen next; later it limits our perceptions and functionally takes over, all this out of conscious awareness. Sadly, sometimes the map is effectively prescribing a life that involves enduring abuse, maintaining passivity, enduring isolation, etc. And so these circumstances occur in the present but relate to experiences the individual endured – and mapped out – at a much younger age.

"Our strongest beliefs were once new and even doubtable conclusions."

Ron Kurtz

Ideally, we should think of the early map as the "first edition," and take every opportunity to revise and update it, applying the learnings culled by life experience and other sources. Or we will hopefully have 'corrective experiences' that help us revise the map. Imagine the distrusting individual who has a relationship that is healing. The map will probably change. But what if the corrective experience doesn't happen? At the end of the day, as Ron Kurtz noted, children make the maps that they will use and rely on as adults. So often, changing the map is a DIY project which has to be undertaken later in life or it won't happen at all. When the effort is expended to read and then change the map, change ensues, bringing new outcomes and opportunities. Now – finally – the world can open up in new ways.

The first step: Peterson argues you need to access your map and so become aware of the values, beliefs and tendencies that drive you. Figure out where the map is pointing you. The ideal that you talk about may be worlds away from the life you are actually living. You may be courting mental health problems as a result.

If your map is off, if your premises, at least some of them, are falsehoods, you might fail where you otherwise would succeed. And if a whole society of people have maps peppered with flawed perceptions and faulty evaluations, society itself can fall into social disarray, tyranny, violence, etc. Sadly, the world has many examples of just how bad things can get. Everybody needs to do their reckoning, to take a good look at the map that they have cultivated and to consider where their map is accurate, and where it is off and potentially leads them astray. Peterson says, "You aim yourself somewhere." Might as well figure out where that is.

Meet Your Map!

Do the personal work and you can find the North on your compass, says Peterson. You need to discover your unique path to live out your own genuine being. But to do this you have to access the map that lurks below, out of conscious awareness. You need to discover what works about your current map and whether antiquated parts of that map need to be updated.

"The Road Less Traveled"

Let's better understand the concept of the map by looking at how Psychiatrist M. Scott Peck described this aspect of human psychology. Back in the 1970's, *The Road Less Traveled: The New Psychology of Love, Traditional Values and Spiritual Growth*, achieved bestseller status, spending 13 years on the New York Times bestseller list. In some ways it was the 70's version of Peterson's *12 Rules*. In it, he articulated ideas that sound like classic Peterson. He wrote about the need for each person to live a life dedicated to the truth. He stated that the person who had a clear perception of reality would be more successful in life, whereas those who failed to understand the contours of reality would make poor decisions and get derailed. For Peck, this perception of reality was a map of life that each person cultivated and used to negotiate reality.

Peck pointed out that people must constantly revise the map they have made so it will remain accurate over time, despite changing circumstances and realities – both internal and external. Peck asserted that many neglect to do so because revising the map is often painful. Refusing to amend and update their map, many will ignore or reject new information, even "crusade" against it, preferring to maintain a narrow and outdated worldview. For Peck, this reluctance to change the map results in many of the ills in society. (Peck, 1978)

Peterson, too, describes the phenomenon whereupon people are reluctant to be corrected if some aspect of their worldview would seem to be flawed. He notes that arguing with someone about a belief they hold dear can prompt a strong angry response, even rage which would seem irrational. After all, why not just admit their mistake and move on?

To quote Peterson on this issue: "when you poke people in the axioms they get upset... Almost like they've been clinging to a raft and you have just pulled out the logs from below and now they will drown . . . why should people be so afraid to move beyond their ideological systems?"

He answers: "we want our protective stories to stay intact. We want to know that our global conceptualizations about reality are accurate and we organize ourselves and our thought structures on that basis. Removing a brick can bring down the whole house." Peck and Peterson agree. It's a painful experience when our conceptualizations are challenged. There are scary implications: What if I can't trust myself as a knower? What if my map is completely wrong?

Peterson reflects, "You have to be laid low before the new revelation can make itself manifest. . . .you have to figure out what's wrong [about your thinking] in order to figure out what guiding wisdom you need to access."

"Enlightenment consists not merely in the seeing of luminous shapes and visions, but in making the darkness visible. The latter procedure is more difficult, and therefore, unpopular."

Carl Jung

As Peterson and Peck understand, the pain associated with new learning is too much for some. Feeling that we have a rational understanding of the world creates a sense of security. And holding certain beliefs may bring another benefit: group identification. Peterson points out that group identification helps us manage the anxiety associated with the unknown aspect of reality. So there are different reasons a person may be reluctant to revise the map of meaning. Another relates to perceptual biases. Interesting research shows the degree to which we will ignore aspects of reality that are not duly noted on our map.

"Believing is Seeing"

If you frequently listen to Peterson, you have heard him describe this study. Students are tasked to watch a short video in which players toss around a basketball. The subjects are told to count how many times the ball is tossed. But there is a catch. There are two teams in the video. The players wearing white are throwing the basketball to others wearing white. There's a team of players wearing black who are throwing another basketball to other players wearing black. The subjects are specifically asked to only count the number of times somebody on the white team throws their ball to somebody on the white team. This task requires more concentration because subjects have to disregard the ball being thrown by and to players wearing black. Subjects complete the task and submit the number of times the ball was tossed. Then they are asked, "did you see the person dressed in the Gorilla outfit?"

Indeed, at one point in the three minute video a tall person walked out wearing a Gorilla costume, thumped his chest a few times and then exited. Subjects were so busy tracking how many times the ball was tossed, they didn't notice the 'gorilla!' Back to Einstein: "Believing is seeing!" Confirmation bias refers to our tendency to only perceive that which we expect. And owing to this human tendency, once you have formed your map of reality, you may not notice anything which contradicts that map.[1]

Peterson points out that those who fail to notice that which disproves their map will usually bear negative consequences – falling into chaos – later. Imagine the person who justifies a vice like smoking. Perhaps his map tells him that he has made many responsible and productive life choices, therefore he is allowed . . no, *deserves* the physical pleasure he gets from smoking. If later this individual experiences a health crisis related to smoking, he may become ill, need treatments or even face death. Had he made a sacrifice when he initially learned of the risks associated with smoking and endured the hardship of breaking the addiction back then, he would have weathered a lesser sacrifice and perhaps avoided a worse sacrifice later.

Any psychotherapist can tell you people are attached to the map that they spent a lifetime using. Our maps influence not just what we say and do, but what we see! It pays to spend the time figuring out where your map is pointing you. As mentioned earlier, all your software and information technology needs to be sporadically updated! If you upgrade your map, you will experience better success in virtually all areas of life. You will experience more stability, a greater feeling of mastery. But if you never 'look under the hood', you may never realize ways your map is out of date and will be unaware of ways you are misperceiving aspects of reality.

But How?

Sure, psychotherapy is a venue for acquiring awareness of the map you have been using to guide you. But what's great about Peterson's work is that he has opened pathways to achieve therapeutic outcomes that don't require paying for help.

Take for example his Self Authoring Suite, an inexpensive program which takes participants through extensive journaling where they can contemplate their life history, their goals and more. As mentioned earlier, Peterson reports that research shows that when first year university students in residence were run through the protocol and did the extensive journaling, the rate of dropouts in first year went down significantly and the marks of the students were higher than those in the control group. Self-contemplation does not have to be done with the aid of a therapist.

Another resource: Peterson has also put together a website where people can fill out a questionnaire and get a report of findings on personality style based on the Five Factor Personality Test. For $10, a person can get a comprehensive report and learn about the degree of introversion or extraversion, neuroses, conscientiousness, agreeableness and other traits that introduce us to ourselves. We get a better idea of the type of person we are relative to others and get some ideas on how we could make changes. For example, the higher the score on a trait called 'neuroses', the more the individual will be helped by cultivating 'conscientiousness'. Getting feedback in the form of tests can help us clarify some of our tendencies while also identifying some of the content of the map of meaning.

Even if you don't do an audit to figure out what your map tells you about life, you can continue to expand your map of reality by reading and learning. Peterson has been extremely generous, putting his many talks and courses on Youtube. Once you start watching his lectures, visit the work of other psychology greats . . . Carl Jung, Milton Erickson, Jay Haley, Jeffrey Zeig, Victor Frankl, James Hillman; the list goes on. The more you learn about psychology or about the world at large by reading or listening to lectures, the more the inner mapmaker integrates new information. You learn new ways of seeing life, new ways of doing, all helping you update your map.

Surely you noticed this already in your studies of Peterson's work. Maybe you started to clean your room, or attend to your self-care regime – cooking, sleep habits, etc. – with more conscientiousness, as you implement his rule to treat yourself with as much care as you would if you were attending to the needs of someone you deeply value. Implementing the Peterson Rules will go a long way in updating that map. And, in so doing you trigger a virtuous cycle makes wherein one positive change spurs the next positive change, and so on. Things get better and better in your life, as opposed to succumbing to the proverbial vicious cycle where things go from bad to worse.

Another way we update the map is by exposing ourselves to classic literature, certain fine works that embed noteworthy lessons, as mentioned above. Perhaps you've been fascinated to watch Peterson analyze stories like Pinnochio or classic fairy tales, to hear him deconstruct the hidden meanings. I'm sure this form of experiencing noteworthy literary works also builds the map in useful ways.

Freshen Up that Map of Yours!

Peterson's message, again and again, is that "you need a path that justifies the tragedy of life." It's just not going to work to rely on that old tired map. Peterson wants us to revisit the map we have been using, to dabble with the unknown, to sway from the old path if it hasn't been working so well. He is our tour guide. Did you know anything about Nietzsche before you read or listened to him? Peterson introduces us to ancestral wisdom and that wisdom can help us make new decisions about how we want to think about life.

Another way he helps us revise our maps is by teaching fundamental principles which describe reality. In an upcoming chapter we summarize some of those core teachings designed to help us better understand the human landscape, so that we can align our map with reality, replacing faulty beliefs with more accurate understandings of reality. First, though, we have to consider our basis for knowing. We will see that over time our means of acquiring knowledge have become skewed, affecting the maps of individuals and society as a whole. Peterson helps us see how, over the last decades, our way of knowing has shifted on a societal level. More specifically, society has taken a nose-dive into unreality and become a breeding ground for flawed ideas or ideologies to take root, making it more difficult to cultivate a solid, useful map of meaning.

Chapter Summary

This chapter details the map of meaning that individuals cultivate at an early age in order to come up with rules which will guide their actions and help them predict outcomes. The map determines how the child will interpret reality and respond to it. We hope over the course of life a person will constantly change and update the original map that they cobbled together in childhood.

Of greatest importance is the fact that these maps are often self-fulfilling. Initially, they are a form of shorthand, letting a child know what life is like so that he or she knows what to expect and how to behave. Later in life, if the map is not updated, the person will find and even create a reality which matches that rendered in that early map. This map, then, may 'aim' the person towards the same hell he or she endured in childhood – even though consciously that lifestyle would be abhorrent to the person. One way a map can prevent new learning is by keeping a person so focused on the negative aspects of reality that were operative in the past, the person will fail to notice exceptions, brighter realities or new choices they can make, even when all of these are presently available.

Given the way the map determines the future, it becomes important to uncover your map, to make that which is unconscious, conscious. You can figure out where the map aims you and decide to change it if that seems necessary.

Sadly, any number of people resist changing the map. They are used to their patterns, unwilling to make changes and experience discomfort if forced to realize flaws in their map. Many would sooner deny the need to change and lie about the true nature of reality, rather than experience the pain of admitting flaws in the map. When this occurs, a person may fall into extreme ideologies, pathology or disastrous outcomes later in life when negative consequences can no longer be staved off.

Peterson advances various methods of uncovering and changing the map. Peterson's journaling exercise is one example.

Reflection Points

Journal the following questions to better integrate some of the ideas in this chapter:

What life experiences do you think affected your map of life? What generalizations about life did you make on the basis of those experiences?

Can you describe the map of one or both of your parents, as you understand it?

In terms of your own map, where are you 'aiming'?

What would you guess would be the beliefs and assumptions that would be central in your map of meaning?

Have certain books, ideas, teachers or other influences triggered you to modify your map of meaning, at any specific points in your life?

Can you identify any errors that might be in your map?

Was there ever a time you learned that your map was incomplete or in need of an upgrade? How did you go about modifying your map?

Have your axioms/assumptions/beliefs changed over the years? Are there beliefs you used to hold by but have subsequently abandoned?

Do you currently harbour any beliefs that you wish you had cause to abandon?

Do you know people who expect life to go a certain way and their predictions seem self-fulfilling? What is the pattern you have observed?

Notes

1. In an often cited quote, 17th century philosopher-scientist Francis Bacon spoke of this human tendency. He wrote, " The human understanding, once it has adopted opinions, either because they were already accepted and believed, or because it likes them, draws everything else to support and agree with them. And though it may meet a greater number and weight of contrary instances, it will, with great and harmful prejudice, ignore or condemn or exclude them by introducing some distinction, in order that the authority of those earlier assumptions may remain intact and unharmed."

4

What's Wrong with Your Map

"It ain't what people know that gives them trouble, it's what they know that ain't so. "

Mark Twain

How do you register reality? Jordan Peterson teaches that we have two different faculties that allow us to know the world. Serving as reservoirs of learning, he refers to them as the explicit declarative memory and the implicit nondeclarative memory.

Explicit declarative memory consists of what we consciously know and can deliberately access and talk about. Explicit memory governs our knowledge of 'what'. By way of example, you can verbally give over everything you know about a given topic.

In contrast, the implicit nondeclarative memory is our knowledge of 'how'. This faculty develops before the other does. It governs sensory-motor function and the process of how we do what we do. It's non-verbal and automated, relating to how we move and other nonverbal tendencies that we cultivated at a very young age. Beyond the 'know how' it stores, this faculty also contains perceptions of reality that we somehow harbour in the body itself. Information or beliefs can be stored out of conscious awareness, as in the expression: 'I knew it in my bones.'

Explicit Declarative Memory	Knowledge acquisition starts once child is verbal	Verbal faculty stores information	Knowledge can be accessed consciously	The domain of 'what'
Implicit Nondeclarative Memory	Behavioural knowledge is acquired when child is preverbal	Non-verbal faculty governs sensori-motor function, stores procedural knowledge	Governs automated patterns for doing, stored in the unconscious	The domain of 'how'

How do you explain why your gait resembles that of your parent? Do you remember deciding to walk like that? Or what about the inner felt sense that something is the right and good thing to do as compared to another action? Some information is embodied, but not understood. And that is the level of knowledge that is often involved in our emotional and behavioural patterns, a product of learnings that we integrated which became 'procedural knowledge'. With regards to personal problems, we often find that our stubborn counterproductive habits have taken root in the subconscious within the implicit faculty. That's why these habits are hard to change. Peterson is going to show us that some of the flawed conceptions or faulty beliefs that trip us up are also locked in that faculty and that they have taken root, at times, thanks to faulty conceptions perpetuated through the culture and society, at large.

We've earlier discussed that culture can, at times, help socialize children by embedding positive values within myths or cultural narratives. But society and culture also sometimes perpetuate negative ideas that we similarly internalize. Let's look at one important example: in contemporary life, science and technology is currently perceived as the language of progress and has become the lens through which we prefer to view our lives and make decisions. Recall that Peterson asserts we are hardwired to learn values and life lessons via the right brain which interprets the unknown and unfamiliar aspects of the world through myths and narratives. He suggests that we best learn how to behave by watching the hero and learn how not to behave by watching the villain. In a society that emphasizes scientific knowledge, though, there is less emphasis on those right brain modalities that he claims most effectively teach how to be a cooperative citizen.

Further and most importantly, Peterson insists the ultimate venue for relating these value laden stories is in the context of a religious tradition. Narratives can present a religious worldview that relays spiritual teachings. For thousands of years, religion was central to most civilizations and only receded in importance with the dawning of the scientific age. Now rationalism discourages us away from 'fairytales' that were guiding narratives in other eras. Richard Rohr conjectures that yesteryear's myths have been replaced with "disorienting narratives like communism, fascism, terrorism, mass production, and its counterpart, consumerism." (Rohr, 2010, Introduction)

He's right. Our current narratives *are* disorienting. In contrast, the narratives from yesteryear created cohesion. People could share a worldview and cooperate, informed by and working within the same value system. In fact, the hardiness of those old-time narratives, which took root in the implicit nondeclarative memory of the earlier generation, is that they continue to influence today's secular society. You could say the religiosity of yesteryear continues to 'off gas', registering as a form of implicit knowledge, although its influence and hold on us gets weaker with time.

"Science takes things apart to see how they work. Religion puts things together to see what they mean."
Rabbi Jonathan Sacks

We've heard the idea 'a fish does not know the water it swims in.' Similarly, we each are steeped in the mentality that characterizes our day and age. We don't realize how we think, what we think, that so many of our premises are a function of the worldview that preceded ours; a worldview that revered divinity and viewed a relationship with the Divine as an essential part of life. Contemporary interest in religion has faded, but we, none the less, bear a faint though discernible influence of our devout ancestors, harbouring implicit knowledge that tells us that doing the right and good thing is important, a notion that emanates more rightly from an earlier era than from our own. In other words, thousands of years of religiosity continues to influence our thinking.

One sign of that influence is a norm whereby people agree that some behaviours are immoral; that there is such a thing as morality. And a secular person may very well argue that his or her sense of morality exists independent of any premise about the existence of a universal god. Yet, from a philosophical point of view, it is hard to defend any particular system of morality as absolutely true and necessarily binding, since one society might have values which differ from another. Some societies might hold that undergoing female genital mutilation is a worthy rite of passage in a particular spiritual system. Without one absolute source that defines what constitutes moral or immoral behaviour, there's really no case to be made that one culture's practices are sacred while another's are barbaric.

Peterson asserts that it is only the premise that humans are made in the image of the Divine that obligates us to revere every human life. That value only wields authority because of the authority from which it came. Today we find ourselves in an era where people have an ethical sensibility as an implicit felt sense but without a relationship to organized religion that inculcates us with higher level teachings, our morality is predicated on the crumbs of our ancestors' piety. We will not be able to perpetuate these values in the generations that come, so weak is our hold on and grasp of the moral sensibility. In other words, we are on our way down, not up.

To review, according to Peterson the religious framework of yesteryear infuses us, permeating our frames of reference on an ethereal level so that it plays a role in our thinking in some sort of hazy way, telling us what we are like, who we are meant to be, what standard we are to live up to. You might think of the attitudes and mentalities of our ancestors serving as a platform on which rests our more modern conceptualization of the world. Their sensibilities are our floorboards. We don't notice them, but they hold us up, at least for now.[1]

How do we see the influence of the religious sensibility as it infuses the secular mentality? If I can introduce some of my own reading at this point, Ann Coulter, author of, *Godless: The Church of Liberalism*, suggests that moderns can discharge the religious impulse of yesteryear by participating in ideologies that serve as substitute religions. She suggests that old-style religion dictates religious rituals whereas the new religion prescribes its own rituals: vegetarianism, recycling, organic gardening, etc. The religions of yesteryear advocated chastity in adolescence and ensconced sexuality as a fixture in marriage only. The new religion construes that teaching children all the permutations of sexual expression is virtuous and normalizes sexuality outside of marriage.

In the religion of yesteryear, members of the clergy perpetuate the tradition by teaching and lecturing. In this new era, Coulter suggests, the high school teachers are the purveyors of the tradition, teaching contemporary ideologies – gender differences are solely a product of nurture, not nature, as one example – always in a school where the Lord's prayer is banned. Coulter holds that the testament of the new religion is 'Roe vs Wade' and its sacrament is abortion. In other words, though the beliefs of the liberal sensibility stand in direct contrast to those at the core of the Judeo-Christian tradition, the fact that there is a priority to uphold values and live in a structure that mimics that of organized religion reflects the imprint of our pious forbearers. As an aside, Peterson, in passing, cited research which suggests that when people perform a "casual moral action" – like recycling as one example – they are prone, subsequently, to justify actions which transgress their standards. It's as if once they have performed a token action that establishes themselves, in their own minds, as morally sound, they permit or justify infractions. Peterson calls this phenomenon, "shallow moralizing."

Let's look at another example. Kathryn Lofton, Assistant Professor of Religious Studies at Yale University, points out that fandom of celebrities is another modern day pseudo-religion. In her book, *Oprah: The Gospel of an Icon*, she also suggests that Oprah and her plethora of products function as a substitute religion. She writes,

> [Oprah] preaches prosperity gospel, she advocates books as scripture, she offers exegesis, she conducts exculpatory rights, she supplies a bazaar of faithful practices, she propagates missions, both home and foreign. She opines repeatedly on the meaning of existeńce, the seat of the soul, the purpose of your life, and the place of a higher calling. Oprah plays religious even as she is, most adamantly (by scholarly classification and by her own), not a religion (Lofton, 2011, p. 9).

Peterson would say that, running on fumes, we have an appetite for ideologies or structures that mimic religion and take us back to old time values. I wonder if that's what motivates constant remakes of old movies, TV series, shows that have younger performers singing the hits of superstars of yesterday. Something compels us to turn back time in a society that otherwise venerates the new and improved. Likely our ancestors spent time each week looking to the root of creation, thinking about who they find there and considering the ramifications for their lives. In contrast, we binge watch old TV series and watch remakes of old movies.

If Peterson, and Nietzsche are right, we are subject to a sensibility that is fading out and once it fades out once and for all, another will emerge, likely one completely divorced from the sensibility of religion. Or religions themselves get corrupted, as suggested by Rohr. He notes that when we abandon healing myths we get "trapped" in destructive myths. [2] Which ever way it goes, it takes us closer to the dissolution of our civilization. Peterson thinks we are gradually floating away from the roots of our civility.

According to Peterson, once we have detached ourselves from a core source of knowledge, the religions that used to inform a level of inner knowledge that is more ephemeral and less articulated, we risk losing our bearings. We will simply come to believe wrong things or attach ourselves to wrong ideas, falling into a sickness of spirit. The only cure, he says, is to integrate a system of belief and representation which will organize the structure of our thoughts. If we don't have a coherent system of belief and representation, we will succumb to disastrous ideologies. Peterson describes these ideologies as "crippled religions . . . like religions but it's missing an arm and a leg… It hobbles along… It gives you some security in terms of group identification but ultimately it is a parasite living on something pure and true."

Another way Peterson expresses it: "when we knock out the slats out of the base of western civilization by destroying this representation – this G-d ideal – we oscillate, moving to the extremes of nihilism and radical or extreme ideologies" Harbouring knowledge and information without that ideal providing a solid base potentially throws us off. The more latent and subtle level of knowing becomes weak, disconnected from higher truths that provide stability. We become dissociated from truth and from our deeper selves. Peterson invites us to find our way back to some form of reverence. He certainly does not advocate any particular religious path. Each can find their own. But he shares works from the various world religions, teaching the wisdom embedded within and hopefully rattling chains so that his readers and listeners will continue reading and learning, all the while wrangling with the ideas that can inform the personal map and help access meaning.

Peterson has dedicated himself to the task of helping a whole generation reconnect with core implicit knowledge, providing bearings that allow a person to better construct a healthy map of reality. He has taken on the fight against a pervading dominant sensibility, armed primarily with classic ideas that people can use to repopulate the inner dimension of knowing.

"The creative artist and poet and saint must fight the actual (as opposed to the ideal) gods of our society – the god of conformism as well as the gods of apathy, material success, and exploitive power. These are the "idols" of our society that are worshiped by multitudes of people."

Rollo May

Chapter Summary

In this chapter, we look at two faculties that Peterson describes which play a role in cognitive functioning: the explicit declarative memory and the implicit non-declarative memory. The explicit faculty stores knowledge that can be expressed verbally. This faculty stores what you know: information. The implicit faculty stores 'know-how': procedural knowledge (how to ride a bike, for example) that is by definition not verbal. We are easily conscious of the information that we have in our explicit declarative memory but will be mostly naïve of the contents of the implicit non-declarative memory.

Peterson argues that nested in the implicit non-declarative memory are important beliefs, values and conceptions which influence how we perceive ourselves and others and which inform our worldview. He asserts that some of the most important learning is that directed to this faculty via myth, narrative and fairy tales. Historically societies used these modalities to imprint young minds with values and learnings that promote civility and cooperation. Yet, in a science-oriented modern world, these modalities have fallen by the wayside. Subsequently, the related faculty is under-developed in young people.

Further, Peterson points out that these modalities have historically been associated with spiritual systems and religions. Using narratives or myths, religions would inculcate a system of morality, a value of human life, even traits such as humility and conscientiousness. Peterson asserts that though society has moved away from religiosity, the values from yesteryear still influence moderns, promoting a moral sensibility and otherwise influencing our standards and how we perceive ourselves. Yet, Peterson suggests that this influence weakens with time. Few are actively engaged in religiosity which would shore up a reverent worldview anchored around morality. Peterson predicts that unless these learnings are reinvigorated, they will truly fade out over the next few decades to the detriment of civilized society. In that case, he predicts more pseudo-religions will emerge and people will affiliate with these substitute religions in an effort to find an anchor, identify with a group and fill the need that results when the G-d ideal is abandoned. When this occurs, extreme ideologies take root as people are disassociated from those higher truths that would otherwise stabilize themselves and society, more generally.

Reflection Points

Please consider or journal the following questions to better integrate the material in this chapter.

Which children's stories made an impression on you when you were a child? What values were embedded in those stories?

Which dominant culture influenced you when you were young? Which of the dominant culture's beliefs or values did you internalize at that young age? Which of those values and beliefs do you still hold by today?

Are there any societal values or beliefs that you had internalized but abandoned or rejected later in life? Are there some beliefs you internalized which you want to retire, but find it difficult to do?

In your life, which patterns have you found difficult to change (suggesting that they took root in the implicit non-declarative memory and therefore serve as automated behaviours that are difficult to change by conscious decision)?

Notes

1. Peterson reflects, "We live on the corpse of our culture . . . but the system has to be revivified." We live in a secular society that has people abandoning religion. The system is not being revivified. Without bona fide religion actively suffusing it, it will fizzle out for good.
2. Seems to me, one example could be the Jihad's understanding that the reward for killing the enemy is access to 72 virgins in Heaven.

5

Peterson's Map of Meaning

As we begin to look at Peterson's core teachings, I'd like to mention Peterson's overriding priority, the task of bringing order to chaos. The second line of Genesis introduces the concept of chaos:

"when the earth was astonishingly empty, with darkness upon the surface of the deep, and the Divine Presence hovered upon the surface of the waters"

That line relates two primary aspects of creation:

> a) a lower dimension which is a 'mass' of empty darkness or as Peterson calls it, " a formless and potential chaos." That chaos will be the matter "from which all things will emerge and rise." Water implies movement. We might expect water to be affected by the hovering movement that occurs above. Depth, emptiness and darkness would seem to imply the absence of order or intelligence.

b) The second constituent of this creation is suspended above the first: the intelligence, the Divine Presence, hovering above. Early in the creation narrative we find the vertical dimension referenced, bringing an association to the hierarchy, but more on that later. With the creation of Adam, the Divinity penetrates the lifeless body, breathing into and so bringing life/order to a lump of clay. Fusing Divinity with physicality has a functional byproduct: the human can stand, speak, name the animals and so mimic the verbal declarative acts of his Creator. Like Father, like son.

As we follow the text, we see that at the outset of any creation, crude physicality always needs tweaking. Each facet of creation is then landscaped, organized, ordered; then it works! Only then is it 'good' by Divine account. The act of fusing the spiritual and the physical will become the universal strategy we use to aim at 'good'. In line 2, though, the Divine is not fused with the creation. He hovers above. Physicality and Divinity are separate. The word good is not associated with this stage of the creation process.

How do things play out? The physical world, as per the last verse, has water covering the entire surface of the world. In order to move past that chaotic state, a process of ordering has to take place. G-d has to clean his room! He pushes the water to the side, making way for land but this only occurs after He separates the upper waters from the lower waters. More ordering!

When the sun and the moon are created, there is chaos. Note that in the text, the sun and the moon are initially described as two great lights. Then Genesis 1:16 continues, "the great light to rule by day and the small light to rule by night." What happened? The Talmud teaches there was a dispute. When you have two great lights there will be an inevitable power struggle. Chaos! G-d subsequently reduced the moon, creating a clear hierarchy that resolved the immediate conflict. [1]

The animals are created. They are ordered when Adam gives them their names. Speech will have a lot to do with how we order the world. Or as Peterson points out, "conscious articulation helps bring something into actualization . . . we can't get a grip of something till it has a name."

You see the pattern every where you look. Wheat in its natural state is not terribly useful. You can't eat it. It takes a lot of processing/ordering to derive value from it. Ever try to bite into a raw rutabaga? It takes serious cooking to make that thing edible. And it took quite a bit of ordering to invent electricity, light bulbs, computers, etc.

What about human development? Initially, as children, we are chaotic! No wonder our early maps of meaning are inadequate! Landscaping is required! We have to sort ourselves out, integrating the influence and intelligence of the Divine Presence, aka the influence of parents, authority figures, teachings, teachers, etc. That presence looms above, overhead, so each person has to look higher on the hierarchy to access somebody that has more clarity, someone who can direct and guide. If we find role models or teachers who will help us access the Divinity that hovers overhead, we can actualize our potential.

We will need principles to guide the ordering task, especially given the baseline chaos that exists. What teachings will help us tame and order the chaos so we can understand reality and master it? I'd like to suggest those principles are the ones Peterson teaches, accounting for the popularity and relevance of his work.

Peterson brings out these core insights in an age characterized by terrible confusion aka chaos. ADHD addles the mind of the young, dementia invades the elderly, gender no longer plays a role in defining our lives. A lot of the markers we used to use to organize life are gone. Remember when all stores were closed on Sundays? Remember when night was a time for sleep because there wasn't much else you could do? Hillman and Ventura (1992) comment, "Twenty-four hour bank call-ins and automatic tellers are in themselves insignificant details of contemporary life. But as part of a pattern, it speaks of a people increasingly coaxed to live without pattern in terms of services, while they bemoan the loss of pattern in their morality, their love-life, their thought...(p. 116)." Contemporary life is disorienting.

The principles that Peterson has been teaching seem to be helping people. He suggests you can use them to cope with chaos and confusion. He claims using these principles can help you "turn chaos into habitable order." Some of these ideas could be called 'common sense'. But he is a breath of fresh air, to bring my Genesis metaphor forward! He gives us a language for all this and then we can stand, like Adam, and name our world! When we do that, we sort ourselves out!

Let's look specifically at some of Peterson's central teachings. If we have integrated faulty understandings about reality into our map/worldview, Peterson "pokes us in the axioms." He challenges our conceptions of reality, triggering insight that can help the project at hand!

The Core Dimensions of Life

To flesh out these ideas, I'd like to present them in a format that is my own. Consider that by the time the Creation narrative is done, the life space has familiar dimensions: vertical, horizontal, field of depth, and if we consider a three dimensional cube as a metaphor for the life space, there is also another dimension: the center point, hidden in the middle of the cube. The center point is situated centrally and equidistant from each of the six sides of the cube. You could say that the cube finds its unity through the center point because it serves as the common point of connection for each side, connecting them all.

I'd like to suggest that so many of Peterson's insights are, at core, intrinsically relevant and true to reality, that we can organize these teachings and show their correspondence to the familiar dimensions of the physical world: depth, width and height. Note that I am putting his learnings in this format, which I think is handy, but that formulation is not one that he discusses in his books or lectures.

The Vertical Axis

According to Peterson, complex biological creatures have to move towards things in the world in order to stay alive. We move towards food, people, experiences that we perceive will make our lives better. The fact that life has us moving forward as we pursue our wants and needs will relate to depth of field, to be discussed soon. But because we reach to achieve goals that we project out into the future, we now have the necessity of hierarchies. Hierarchies relate to the vertical dimension of life.

We said earlier that there is a hierarchy of value. Some things are worth pursuing and other outcomes are best avoided. The positive aspect of living with hierarchies is that we have the possibility of aiming at and achieving desirable outcomes. If there is a higher goal, there is also a less attractive alternative. When people have something to aspire to, their lives have meaning. With no outcome to strive towards, life feels useless. So in many ways the hierarchy adds quality to our lives.

But hierarchies introduce their own set of problems. Inevitably, a small group of people will find their way to the top of the hierarchy, say, of competence, while the majority will be dispossessed, marginalized at the bottom, caught up in less favourable circumstances. Further, there is the potential that those at the top abuse their power, resulting in tyranny. So hierarchies come with imperfect outcomes. Peterson points out we have to monitor the more unfortunate and inevitable negatives which come into play when dealing with hierarchies.

In his book, *12 Rules for Life*, Peterson writes one chapter about the topic of hierarchies and calls his rule on the topic, "stand up straight with your shoulders back." Indeed, standing up straight has a person inhabiting the vertical axis. The person who stands up straight will exert self-discipline and governance in other aspects of life, too. He or she tries harder, putting in the extra effort to "climb the corporate ladder" or other ladders of competence. The vertical dimension is an inevitable part of the landscape and he who submits to that fact will set high goals, cultivate role models, and healthy relationships to authority figures. We expect more wins for these people. Next we can consider the horizontal axis.

The Horizontal Axis

If we think about the body, we can notice that forward movement, walking, requires alternating movements between the right and left side of the body; you have to put the right foot forward, followed by the left, and so on. The vertical axis would have us reach for the stars, way up there, but the horizontal axis, to keep us grounded, wants us to deploy both faculties, the right and the left, sequentially, to stay grounded.

When Peterson talks about the horizontal axis – right and left – he is talking about political orientation/temperament. It's no coincidence that right wing and left wing imply something spatial and more specifically relating to a body, as in the wings of a bird. In fact, these two orientations represent the extremes along a continuum that I am calling the horizontal axis. Along these lines, some mystical traditions locate different tendencies in the personality in different parts of the body; the left and right axis relate to a continuum which has expansive, creative generosity at one end of the spectrum and contractive, legalistic tendencies at the other end. In common parlance, we refer to these polarities as extroversion and introversion. One could argue that every personality needs to master both of these capacities or orientations, while also recognizing that each person will have more of one than the other.

According to Peterson, the right wing is a political orientation that values hierarchies and focuses conscientiously to implement them. The left-wing sensibility offers checks and balances, vigilant to inequities that can occur when hierarchies exist. This group is sensitive to the plight of those who are marginalized at the bottom of the hierarchy and alert to potential abuse of power at the top of the hierarchy. If the right wing is unfettered, tyranny can result. On the other hand, if the left-wing is unchecked the hierarchy is eroded under policies which favour the marginalized but the economic viability of the state may be tested.

Peterson describes the primary psychological traits that research associates with members of each group. The right wing is characterized by "conscientiousness," which includes sub-traits like orderliness, logical thinking and a tendency to be highly responsible. Skilled at limit-setting, this personality is risk averse, always mindful of what can happen when boundaries are not maintained. This type possesses excellent executive skills and so is drawn to roles such as manager or administrator.

"Openness" is the trait that corresponds to the left-wing mentality. This personality is creative, potentially rebellious and motivated to innovate new protocols and hierarchies, the classic entrepreneur type. Society needs both types to thrive, asserts Peterson, but they best function in dynamic dialogue versus pitted against each other in a highly polarized tug-of-war.

"If we can stay with the tension of opposites long enough – sustain it, be true to it – we can sometimes become vessels within which the divine opposites come together and give birth to a new reality."
Marie-Louise von Franz

With regards to the horizontal axis, we can appreciate there are two disparate faculties that each person possesses, and even if each person has a favored way of approaching the world, we need to deploy sometimes one, sometimes the other. We have to view both faculties as important and necessary for the human project to succeed. Walking is the metaphor that represents the harmonic function of both faculties working in synch to move things forward. In fact, The proper execution of the two disparate aspects of self, which has them both developed and executed in a way that is inspired, is the goal of alchemy. This is the topic of volume 2 of this series, called, *Maps of Meaning: An Illustrated Guide for Using Jordan Peterson's Insights on Divinity to Sort Yourself Out,* to be released in September 2019.

Depth of Field

The depth of the cube introduces the dynamic of living in the context of time. Note that we understand time spatially. The past seems to be behind us, the future before us. Think of life as requiring us to navigate the space between the center point (representing the present, where you are right now) and a point forward in the future, moving you 'out there'. Will we focus on instant gratification and therefore be stuck in an eternal, unchanging present? Or will we live with a future orientation? Peterson tells us "not to sacrifice who we could be for who we are right now." Better to spend time and energy today to accomplish some objective in the future. Or, as he advises us, "Take your future self into account."

This idea takes us back to our original premise: reality is not a world of things. Reality is a world of action. At any given moment we have our current state in the present and a more desired state which lives, at least in our imagination, in the future. Living properly in the depth of field/ the framework of time, requires us to take purposeful action; in so doing we create a meaningful life. Culture, mythology, popular fairytales and biblical stories introduce us to the archetype of the hero, the one who delays gratification and purposely takes decisive action in order to achieve a desirable goal.

"The smallest good act today is the capture of a strategic point from which, a few months later, you may be able to go on to victories you never dreamed of."
CS Lewis

Once we understand that action is necessary, we have to determine what kind of action to take. Note that the Asian classic, *Tao Te Ching,* translated as the "Classic of the Way's Virtues," is an Eastern guide to practices and life choices that constitute the ideal 'way' of being or behaving. The Tao itself refers to a cosmic universal pattern which animates the superior 'way', hence it is referred to as 'the way'. In another ancient tradition, Jewish law is called "*Halacha*" in Hebrew, derived from the word "h*olech*," the Hebrew word for 'walk'. Jewish law, then, proscribes a way of walking, a way of progressing. Peterson notes that all religions prescribe their version of the ideal way to advance in life. This allows us to move through time with more direction, while maintaining ourselves purposefully on the straight and narrow.

Why straight? Straightness is a virtue in the sacred traditions compared to the gentle curves that characterize nature. Think about it. If you stand on a curved road, you look behind you and you can't see where you've come from. You look before you and you can't see where you're going. Straightness represents alignment (find the line in there?) of speech, deed and heart. Within the line we find the 'I', the organized experience of selfhood, finding "oneself," or 'one self', the healthy, unified identity, the prototype of psychological health. [2]

The Center Point

Rumi said, "Yesterday I was clever, so I wanted to change the world. Today I am wise, so I am changing myself." There is a story told of Rabbi Israel Salantar, a sage who said that when he was young he first decided that he wanted to change the world, then downgraded, resolving to change his city, then his family. Ultimately he set his sights on the only thing he could change, himself.

Peterson advances the above-mentioned idea and issues the battle cry to the young: "Clean your room!" He understands that young people see many problems in the world and, compelled by idealism and the energy of youth, can charge into the task of 'changing the world'. But there is a problem. World problems are much bigger than any given 20 year old! And further, "it is easier for things to go really wrong than it is for them to go right." Implementing so called global 'solutions' can have all sorts of unanticipated negative consequences.

Given all the barriers, Peterson has a better idea: change your own "local landscape." Fix what is right in front of you! Your room, your field of being, "which is an externalization of your mind," notes Peterson. Get rid of the rubbish! Straighten up what you can straighten up! Organizing your room organizes your psyche, says Peterson. It makes you more effective, overall, maybe even makes you better at work or slightly more useful to your family. So don't fix the world! "Fix what is in your domain of competence," he says. "Build a microcosm of perfection with what you have at hand."

Then he adds, maybe, once you have gone through all your stuff – and now you know how hard it is to do one simple project from start to finish – only at that point do you hesitantly "extend a tentacle out beyond [your little life space] and tap something in the real world [to try to change it] . . . gently!!" Good advice about how to live in the center point, the sweet spot of your reality.

Note that we are all ideally treading paradox. As per above, we are to live in the depth of field which means we are always to have a future focus. We should be looking around and seeing what is wrong in the world and what needs to be fixed. But at the same time, we need to be anchored in the center point. First, fix yourself! Don't get lost in the depth of field, shooting yourself out into the environs to fix everybody else. Start with self-repair! And conversely, once you sort yourself out, then you further extend into the 'depth of field'. Maybe there's something in the world out there that you really can change. Don't only live in the center point! And don't only throw yourself wildly forward traversing the depth of field but oblivious to what is near at hand that needs to be managed! The complexity of living!

Take Care of Yourself

Another Peterson principle that relates to the center point is the idea that you should treat yourself like you would treat somebody whom you value. When he comes up with this idea, he is tackling what we might call a masochism that quietly plays a part of the culture. Perhaps born of the Protestant work ethic, some people have a tendency to self-deny.

Your blood sugar is falling, or you really have to go to the bathroom, but the impulse is, "let me just finish this task." It truly is bedtime. You can't keep your eyes open. But you push forward, "let me just finish this." By the time you finish, the adrenaline has kicked in. Now you are wide-awake. What do you do? Maybe get more work done. Or take a sleeping pill. Neither is the good way to go.

Making the right choice from the position of the center point means factoring the body's experience and best interests into decisions you make at any moment of decision. Peterson knows that there is a tendency to self-neglect. He writes a chapter of the *12 Rules* book so as to help you notice the pattern, catch it, and make new decisions that enhance your life and your experience of well-being. When you make responsible decisions in the center point, the here and now, you keep yourself in good form so you are in shape to exert and work towards your goals, as they relate to the vertical axis mentioned earlier.

The Teachings

It seems to me that some of Peterson's most important teachings pertain to the above mentioned aspects of life (and this certainly is not an exhaustive list). In his work, Peterson analyses many fairytales, movies, creation myths, classic literary works, all to demonstrate the teachings that are embedded within each narrative. These teachings are accessed by the less conscious self when reading these works, but are brought to our conscious awareness when Peterson points out the various metaphors and hidden meanings embedded in each story. If we populate our personal life maps with these ideas, our lives will be better for it.

Chapter Summary

In this chapter, we reviewed some of Peterson's core teachings and categorized each to one of the 'dimensions' of the physical universe: height, width, depth of field and the center point. I suggested that Peterson's teachings are so fundamental to physical existence that each relates to one aspect of the physical world or another. These are fundamental concepts we can use to understand and interpret reality and to turn chaos into order.

Peterson talks at length about the hierarchy associated with the vertical dimension of this world. Since ours is a world of value, any action or goal or behaviour falls somewhere on a hierarchy. Some outcomes will equate with success whereas others assume a place lower in the hierarchy, resulting in a less favourable outcome. Peterson asserts that those who 'climb the ladder of competence,' those who 'aim high', will find meaning in life.

He also points out that the hierarchy is going to result in inequality. In a world where some achieve success, others will not. Society must have checks and balances in place to help the unfortunate. Society cannot banish the hierarchy, though, because the hierarchy is necessary; it helps people establish goals and secure meaning in life.

Another dimension of physical space, the horizontal dimension, associates with Peterson's ideas about left and right. He is discussing a polarity where people assume a place at one end of the spectrum or another, expressed in their political attitudes and also their personality traits. People on one side of the spectrum, 'the right-wing', have an overriding trait of conscientiousness and are extremely mindful about protecting borders and boundaries. People on the other side of the spectrum have an overriding trait that Peterson calls "openness" which corresponds to creativity and out-of-the-box thinking. Those on the 'left' aspire to innovate, spur progress and dissolve boundaries, in so doing. A functional society rightly engages the input of both sensibilities. Both perspectives are necessary to move society forward.

The third dimension of physical space is depth of field. In our normal consciousness, we locate the past behind us and the future, before us.

Life has us moving through time . . .and space. Time, therefore, is represented by depth of field. Peterson argues that to live successfully we have to properly orient ourselves somewhere between the present and the future. People entrenched in the present are prone to addictions and disengaged from goals. People who neglect the present, hyper-focussed on future goals may experience health problems or social isolation as life assumes a driven quality. Engaging adequately with the present (the centre point) while simultaneously investing in the future, is an art form. To do this, people must put thought into how to live. Religious models and spiritual systems usually teach their own systems for living in an effort to teach adherents how to live well.

The center point associates with the present moment. Peterson anchors us to the present moment by urging us to 'clean our rooms' or to treat ourselves like we would treat people we value. Both of these directives require us to properly care for our space, our physical needs and attend conscientiously to our immediate circumstances.

Peterson's core teachings are useful because they speak to the core aspects of our physical existence in a very existential way, perhaps accounting for the popularity of his work.

Reflection Points

Journal or reflect on some of these questions to better integrate the material in this chapter:

What is your life like when you're under stress and experiencing chaos? How has chaos historically played out in your life when things have not been going well?

When you are on your game and properly ordering your life, what actions are you taking? How are you living?

In terms of the vertical axis of life, what goals are you 'aiming' towards?

In terms of the horizontal axis, do you identify yourself as more aligned with the 'left' or 'right' sensibility? What could you do to develop the sensibility/traits associated with the opposite polarity so as to better balance your personality?

Depth of field: are there wisdom teachings that you implemented now or in the past which helped you determine how to act in life? Have these teachings been a help to you or a deterrent?

Rate your alignment of speech, deed and heart. Do you move in a consistent direction (as a rule) or are you, at times, erratic?

Do you have a history of self-sabotage? If you ever sabotaged your own goals, how did you do this? What rules did you subsequently implement to prevent this from happening again?

Center point: is your "local landscape" in good shape? If you took on cleaning your room, what would be the first step?

Do you take proper care of yourself or are you prone to neglecting self-care? What first steps would help you change that pattern?

Notes

1. Note that even G-d Himself recognized that this move was problematic; that He was guilty of a misdeed for imposing this power differential. Somehow reducing the station of the moon was still warranted for the betterment of the world's function. There are many

sources that discuss this issue, which is not a matter of concern here but may be a topic for discussion in a later volume

2. These are ideas I heard articulated by Rabbi Dr. Akiva Tatz in his online lectures.

Part 2

6

Memories Show Where You're 'Aiming'

Part 1 of this book presents central Peterson concepts including that of the 'map of meaning' as well as other insights that relate to reality and how we perceive it. Readers who are primarily interested to understand Peterson's central ideas might limit their reading to Part 1.

In Part 2, I'd like to introduce a method developed by Alfred Adler, MD. Adler discovered that by collecting and analyzing the 10 Early Recollections of psychotherapy clients, he could discern what he called the 'life style' of the client, what Peterson calls the 'map of meaning'. The following chapters will demonstrate Adler's technique in order to more fully teach and exemplify the map of meaning. This work demonstrates – in a very practical way – how that map manifests. Readers who wish to better understand the map of meaning in an applied sense will benefit from working with the material that follows.

What follows are directions that you can use yourself or give to family and friends so as to have them prepare a list of their 10 earliest memories. The best way to learn how to analyze memories is by playing with the technique. I encourage you to collect the series of memories from various people you know and use some of the principles demonstrated and described in the next few chapters in order to analyze them. If you work directly with the map of meaning, spending time discerning it, you may acquire a skill which promotes insight and ultimately aids the understanding of self and others. Part 2 of this book, then, is for those who would like to get some hands-on experience better understanding the map of meaning by working with material that people can submit which reveals it. Consider, though, that analyzing early memories involves cracking the code, learning the language of the unconscious mind. Learning any new language takes time and energy. I present this material because I find it fascinating. Those who enjoy interpreting art, dreams or novels will enjoy extending their analytical efforts in this new direction.

With regards to the directions that follow, you may write down your 10 earliest memories and, upon completing the book, see if you are able to find patterns that reveal your map of meaning. If, though, you are unable to identify patterns, there are additional books that you can read on this subject, one of which is listed in the Recommended Reading section. Additionally, Adlerian psychotherapists are specifically trained in the skill of interpreting memories. You can locate a practitioner for consultation and this clinician can interpret the memories and discuss your life style with you.

As a rule, the more you work with memories, the more you will be able to decode the interesting patterns they reveal. A motivated learner will collect memories from friends and family and work with each individual to contemplate the series of memories while considering the patterns they reveal. Interpreting memories and learning the mysterious language of the psyche is a fascinating venture. Come for the ride, if the idea intrigues you.

Why it Works?

Adler's Earliest Recollection Test requires that the individual writes down his or her 10 earliest memories, each being the recollection of an event that happened once. One is not to use general memories such as, "we used to go to the beach." You might wonder why analyzing a few memories could access much of anything beyond a history of events in the past.

Let's revisit what the Adlerian's say about life style and memory: a young child needs to come up with a map of life. Each child will cultivate generalizations or expectancy sets. What can I expect of teachers? Women? Myself? If you think about it, the exercise of coming up with a rudimentary map would best be accomplished by using the intellect. The trouble is that in childhood we lack a sophisticated, fully-formed intellect. Yet, if we don't come up with a map of life, we are going to be confused and potentially anxious in virtually every situation. We would find ourselves disadvantaged, without a clue as to what to expect in different situations. Having a map gives us a rough idea of what will happen in novel situations, letting us bring learnings of the past to bear on the present: "In my life so far, most kids are like *x*. So this kid is probably going to be like *x*, as well."

We have to come up with some kind of map. It's going to be imperfect and we are going to (hopefully) keep revising that map when some of our earlier generalizations prove inaccurate. But how do we make this map when the undeveloped intellect of a child cannot functionally help? Under the circumstances, the right brain, in charge of pattern recognition and deciphering novelty/negotiating the world of chaos, comes to the rescue. Remember: the right brain is not verbal. The currency of the left brain is words. The currency of the right brain is memory; visual pictures that impressionistically render and preserve the *gestalt* of what happened. That's about all it has to work with.

The subconscious will keep certain memories at the top of the mind, very available and accessible, while other memories which are construed as unimportant or irrelevant will fall away, quickly forgotten. Those memories that are retained will serve as silent reminders, quietly perpetuating beliefs and learnings, whispers from the back of the mind which say: "life is like this." "This is what you can expect." And those memories will sit, primed, reminding you of your map but, as the right brain is nonverbal, will remain out of conscious awareness. There's that implicit memory we have been discussing!

And what's even more interesting is that these memories are easily and readily available to us, easily retrieved. Most people can write them down. This becomes our starting point. Let's look at an example and see how the technique can play out when using it to analyze an early memory of a public figure.

Remembering Joan Rivers

Joan Rivers, the late comedian, wrote several books over the course of her life, including two autobiographies. One detailed the story of her childhood. She documented the strife of her parents' marriage. In the book, she mentions the earliest memory of her mother and the earliest memory of her father. What we are going to see is the degree to which those first memories – even without the other nine that we would ideally collect if we were administering the Earliest Recollections Test – are rife full of predictive power. Let's look.

Joan Rivers' mother grew up with great affluence; later, the family was impoverished. Her first memory had her in her crib, and her mother, an active socialite, came in to kiss her daughter good night before leaving for the evening. In this memory, Joan's mother reaches for the elegant mink stole, feeling the luxurious sensation of the fur as her mother withdraws from the kiss. The vivid part of the memory is the rich sensuality, the tactile pleasure associated with the feel of the garment.

Her father's background: in Europe, his family was destitute. They could barely make ends meet. In his memory, his mother was cobbling together a few pennies by selling oranges on the street. In this memory, Joan's father stood by, a young child watching impotently as a police officer came over to his mother and demanded to see a permit. She did not have a permit to sell those oranges. He confiscated her produce. She wailed. He was helpless. This was his trauma. He went to medical school, practiced as a physician (though lacked business acumen) and lived in dire fear of poverty. From that memory alone we might deduce that he had a form of posttraumatic stress. He was ever vigilant, afraid to spend. Then consider who he married. Yikes!

Analyzing Joan's mother's memory, we see that this first memory is about mother . . . leaving! Analyzing this memory we conclude/ conjecture that there was distance between Joan's mother and Joan's grandmother. After all, the first memory represents the separation of mother and daughter! Mother is leaving. Whose first memory is that of mother *leaving*? If the relationship was characterized by distance, what we might be seeing here is a child who comes to equate the experience of luxury as a mother substitute. Saying that is a way of alluding to an addictive relationship with material possessions. Joan later quipped about her mother, "elegance was her religion" (Bennetts, 2016, p. 26). We have addressed the topic of pseudo-religions in an earlier chapter.

Indeed, the life these two parents lived was in sync with their earliest memories. Joan's mother was on an endless quest to secure every sign of affluence despite the protests of her husband who cried poverty. In one major conflict, Joan's mother took her to the fur district and spent $2000 (this being many decades ago) on a fur coat. They brought the coat home. That night her parents fought the fight of all fights.

Joan's mother would spontaneously buy new furniture and possessions, grasping every sign of affluence. Her father would fight, cry poverty, run out of money when they were on vacations. The marriage dissolved into stony silence punctuated by warfare; all this was an expression of their core issues as we see them depicted in the earliest memories of each. Her father lived a life where the oranges were plucked away from him . . . by his wife. Her mother lived a life where she, again and again, grabbed the fur, the furniture, the opulence, to no end, to no satiation point. And so their lives and their marriage was reduced to the dynamics that were depicted so clearly in those early memories.

And this is what Peterson and Adler both point out. The map you cobble together in childhood and use to interpret reality becomes predictive. You will attract people and situations into your life so as to prove your map to be correct! Why would Joan's father marry someone who valued opulence above all? Because his crude map, formed under conditions of trauma, was all he had guiding him! The map told him: this is what life is like! He found the person who would make a life that matched these expectations! She was the policeman, confiscating the oranges! And he was the mother withdrawing, giving his wife brief pleasurable sensations associated with the goodies that money can buy but withdrawn emotionally. As Einstein said, "Believing is Seeing." We will find more of the same, more of what we experienced already, because that is all we know.

How to Collect the Memories

There are directions for properly documenting the 10 earliest memories.

I tell clients:

> "Please write down the 10 earliest memories you have from childhood. Let's define a memory as something that happened once. If that's the case, you cannot use the memory of swimming on the beach as one of your earliest memories because that is not a specific memory. These 10 memories need to be memories that document events that happened once and once only.
>
> You are not to use photographs to prime your memory. The idea here is that we wish to collect the earliest memories that occur to you spontaneously, those sitting at the top of the mind, as it were, available to you when you ponder your childhood. Ideally we are looking for memories before age 8. Having said that, if you don't have memories from before age 8, then we will accept memories from adolescence or just the earliest memories that you have.

For some people who have experienced trauma, they may find that reviewing old memories is too traumatic and flares up anxiety symptoms. When this is the case, I request that people do not write down their 10 earliest memories. Instead, I ask people to write down 10 memories of highly specific movie moments (or scenes from television shows) that they recall (but not moments from last night's tv watching. The memories need to be from long ago, ideally). In other words, the memories don't have to be from their own childhood. This allows us to avoid the risk of re-traumatizing certain people who have painful early memories. If reviewing your early memories will awaken negative feeling states please do not use your own memories when doing this exercise.

In terms of documenting the memories, people should provide as much detail as possible for each memory, maybe a couple of paragraphs for each. The memories should be written one by one as they occur to the individual. Write them in the order that they come to mind. Don't put them in chronological order. The order that they occur to you is more important than the chronological order.

Once a person writes a couple of paragraphs documenting the memory, they should take a guess their age at the time of the memory and write down two other headings: vivid moment and vivid feeling.

Imagine the memory itself as a movie where a few things happened culminating in some end result. That we will call the memory proper. Once a person recounts the sequence of events in that memory, they need to jot down the moment to which he or she is most associated when they think of that memory. I'm going to call that the vivid moment. If we represented the memory as a movie, we would represent the vivid moment as the freeze-frame. You can ask, "if you had to choose just one, what part of that memory is most vivid?" Next they need to write the vivid feeling that he or she had then, at that vivid moment. Happy? Bored? Frustrated?

So to summarize, a person thinks of the first memory and writes it down in as much detail as possible, one or two paragraphs, and also guessing his or her age in that memory. Next he or she writes: vivid moment, recording the vivid moment. Underneath that: documenting the 'vivid feeling' experienced at that vivid moment. The test involves doing that protocol 10 times, each time collecting a different early memory. Tell your subject not to rearrange the order of the memories. You want the memories in the order they come to mind.

Next we will look at a series of memories to see how they reveal the map of meaning.

7

A Case Study

Interpreting the memories of others allows you to see the narrative that emerges when the subconscious tosses up one memory after another. In this chapter, I introduce you to Steve, a former client (not his real name) who gave me permission to write his story. I'd like you to review and think about his 10 memories. In the next chapter, we will analyze them in detail.

Meet Steve

Many years ago a man in his 30's called me, having been referred for psychotherapy to address his problem with "perfectionism." On the phone, he told me that he found it hard to get things done. He would fixate on the long list of all he had to achieve, ruminating and procrastinating. When we sat in person, though, he confessed to more serious problems. He was in a relationship but had not told his girlfriend that he was not capable of monogamy; he routinely had trysts of which she was not aware. He was smoking marijuana five times a day and had been doing so for the last 20 years. His girlfriend knew about that habit but did not know that he was also doing cocaine. He smoked cigarettes and worked out extensively. He worked in the hospitality industry and, as a very handsome man, easily met women. He was living a double life, knowing his life partner would not approve of his secret lifestyle.

Psychotherapists usually know who they will work well with, and who not. With regards to this client, I was not hopeful.

When I had earlier spoke with Steve on the phone, I had offered him a projective assessment, the process that I often undertake when a client expresses interest in therapy. Clients submit materials that they put together at home; I analyze them. Those materials include the 10 early memories but, in fact, there are many samples of behavior which can be analyzed to understand personality and the psyche. So when I thought that this fellow was struggling with perfectionism, I had offered to do this assessment. He had dutifully prepared materials – writing down recent dreams, doing the drawings I asked for, writing down 'projective' stories, and providing me with a handwriting sample. Handwriting analysis, as an aside, is a projective technique for assessing personality, one that is widely used in Europe (Poizner, 2012).

I was now in a quandry. I thought that Steve required specialized treatment for his addictions and wished to refer him elsewhere. But, because I had offered him a projective assessment, and because he had gone to the trouble to assemble all the needed materials, I gave him two options: he could leave our session and pay nothing, pursuing the referral for drug addiction that I would provide. Or I could do the assessment but he would know that I would not work with him further and then he could pursue that referral.

"Actually, I would like the assessment;" he said. He was curious what would come of it.

We did it. Below you are going to read his 10 earliest memories. Please read them now and jot down any impressions of personality, beliefs, the 'map of meaning', on the basis of those memories. After you put together your thoughts, you can read my interpretations. See if you can get a feeling how these memories might be interpreted before you read the next chapter.

Steve's Earliest Recollections

1. Ghost in closet
Vivid moment: calling for help
Vivid feeling: fear

2. Hospital emergency room after three-story fall
Vivid moment: doctors and nurses fussing
Vivid feeling: pain

3. Dad's friend with cleft chin
Vivid moment: asking if he made it with a pencil
Vivid feeling: curious

4. Nap time at kindergarten
Vivid moment: seeing other children lying down
Vivid feeling: contentment

5. Losing my balloons after carnival
Vivid moment: watching them drift to the sky
Vivid feeling: anger, pain

6. Being sexually abused by best friend
Vivid moment: storage locker, under bed
Vivid feeling: confusion

7. Grade 1, student throwing rock in my ear
Vivid moment: my teacher trying to get it out
Vivid feeling: embarrassment

8. Telling my mother that I met a policeman who let me play with gun
Vivid moment: moms disbelief
Vivid feeling: astonishment

9. Neighbors in building being robbed
Vivid moment: footprints in back driveway
Vivid feeling: uneasy excitement

10. Halloween party at first public school
Vivid moment: the haunted house
Vivid feeling: total fear

Your thoughts?

Jot down some notes, impressions and themes that seem to reveal something about Steve. In the next chapter, I take you through these memories in great detail, so we can see the map of meaning that they reveal.

8

Case Study: The Reveal

"The real voyage of discovery consists not in seeking new landscapes, but in having new eyes."

Marcel Proust

Time for our reveal. Now we look close up not only at the content of the memories, but even consider the format. The latter will be our starting point.

Format of Memories

Let's start by looking at the format of the memories. I give everybody the same directions in terms of how to put together these early memories. I always explain that I would like a couple of paragraphs about each memory. What does it mean if I give those directions and the person gives me back the most abbreviated, minimalistic accounting of the memories? That's what Steve did.

On one hand, it's a sign of intelligence. This is somebody who abstracts the most important concept and renders *that.* On the other hand, it indicates independent-mindedness and rebellion. Recall, I do tell people to write as much as possible about each memory. This is somebody who does not quickly bow to authority! This is the guy who makes his own rules. He decides. So that's the first thing we deduce.

That was absolutely true about Steve!

IF you did the exercise yourself, you can look at your own memories and see how you did it. If each memory goes on for many paragraphs then you may be the person who overworks. Could it be that you second-guess yourself so that when you are performing a task you doubt your own competence and overdo, which takes extra time, is tiring and is not an efficient use of time and energy? Your map may tell you that you are functionally not a very good 'doer' which spins you into anxiety about anything you do, and prompts you to keep working on something long after you have reached the required standard.

Or maybe you didn't exactly follow the directions. Instead of writing out a vivid moment for each one, you underlined the vivid moment. You show us your interest in efficiencies and shortcuts, a sign of practical intelligence.

Perhaps you loyally followed the directions. Your memories are organized and they follow the format that has been prescribed, indicating a comfortable relationship with authority. You are well able to follow procedures. You have good executive skills and are happy playing administrative roles. You work comfortably within structures and can design structures and protocols, as well.

Does anything in particular stand out in the way that you completed this exercise? Consider whether it shows us something about you and how you typically do things. Of course, when making interpretations, anything we come up with is speculative. As a therapist analyzing memories, I come up with a hypothesis, and later ask the analysee for feedback. "Is that so about you? Does that make sense?"

Looking at the First Memory

In an earlier chapter, we looked at the first memories of Joan Rivers' parents. We saw one of the important principles about analyzing early memories: if you only have the person's very first memory, you have a lot. The person's very first memory encodes organizing ideas and beliefs. In order to further demonstrate how this works, I want to detour away from Steve's memories for a minute and look at another example: the first memory of the late writer/celebrity, Carrie Fisher.

Carrie Fisher described her earliest memory in autobiographies she wrote. She's about 3 years old, and was staring at a television, watching her mother, Debbie Fisher, acting in a movie. The vivid scene for her is when her mother and the male love interest are about to kiss. The moment deviates from a normal kiss to one where the male awkwardly and surprisingly kisses her mother on the head. Carrie describes watching that moment and feeling embarrassed and humiliated for her mother.

Think about what is encoded in this first memory. The fact that the first memory is not of mother but of mother represented on a TV screen as a character in a movie might imply that she didn't have that much access to her mother in real time. And if you went with that interpretation, you would be right. She and her brother had so little contact with their mother who worked long days making movies that they both made a point of sleeping in the room with her and the stepfather every night – even though the stepfather was sleeping without underwear with his genitalia in plain view.

What of the disconnect represented in the scene in the movie? Can we generalize what she sees on TV as a theme in her map of meaning? That male and female, in romantic situations, don't have a comfortable fit with each other. There will always be a mismatch, a disconnect. Could we conclude that central to her map of life is the idea that male and female do not come together in harmony? Indeed, her mother had three failed marriages. And Carrie was bereft of ongoing contact with her dad who left when she was about 3. She did not experience his acceptance and involvement. Yes, this was part of her map. Her own romantic relationships were unsuccessful.

What of the fact that the first memory has her watching versus doing? This would seem to indicate a person whose primary orientation is visual so her emphasis is on how things look, a recipe for self-consciousness. We predict she will always have one of her eyes, metaphorically speaking, on the wall, watching herself. And the memory indicates that she is quick to conclude that something terrible has happened which reflects badly on the female (here, her mother, her role model). Can we speculate that in relationship she will quickly move to a position where she concludes that she has done something terribly wrong? Yes, that's a reasonable assumption. Indeed, all of these ideas were part of her map of meaning.

In 2016, she published her book, *The Princess Diarist*, sharing the journals that she kept over the course of filming the first Star Wars movie. She disclosed that during that time frame, she was having an affair with Harrison Ford, her costar, who was 18 years older and married. It was a secret relationship and sexual, in nature. She was awash in shame, constantly feeling hungry for his affections and interpreting his nonverbal style as disdain and disinterest. She longed for acceptance, knew the relationship was fundamentally unhealthy and yet committed to it, all the while holding herself in contempt for doing so.

Her poems at the time, easily expressing her map, shows everything we see in that first memory: the mismatch, the style of watching herself steadily and constantly all the while passing negative judgments about herself and being locked in her own head. She knows the relationship is a mismatch, but she continues to pursue it. When the trusted map says that the only relationship to be had is one characterized by mismatch, that is what a person will pursue! I always tell clients, people follow bad maps very carefully!

The stanzas painfully detail her isolation in relationship, reflecting her obsession with the noncommitted and disinterested lover and then conclude, "And there is no one as far past caring/ As he who just doesn't care/ I've washed that man right into my hair." (Fisher, 2016, p. 122)

So Carrie Fisher's earliest memory portends what will happen later. When we look at Steve's earliest memory we see a moment that stands diametrically opposed to the muscular handsome man who looked so confident and able in person. Steve's memory, featuring him afraid of the ghost in the cupboard, denotes vulnerability, a childish imagination and a tendency to experience anxiety. We conjecture a lack of male support and involvement in his childhood, little access to a father who would teach courage in the face of fear.

We conjecture that the macho demeanor he radiates day-to-day is an act, covering up for the guy who needs help to get his bearings as a male. And note that there is not even one memory with his dad actively in the moment with him. Where is his dad?

Looking at the First Three Memories

Next let's look at the first three memories as a unit. In my experience, the first two memories show two different considerations, primary ideas about the self or the world, sometimes ideas which are juxtaposed against each other. The third memory often reveals how the subconscious resolves the tension between the first two aforementioned perspectives. Read Steve's first 3 memories with this idea in mind.

1. Ghost in closet
vivid moment: calling for help
vivid feeling: fear

2. Hospital emergency room after three-story fall
vivid moment: doctors and nurses fussing
vivid feeling: pain

3. Dad's friend with cleft chin
vivid moment: asking if he made it with a pencil
vivid feeling: curious

First 3 Memories Interpreted

We could say that the first memory shows the idea that this individual is childish. He is afraid of the ghost! The second memory would seem to indicate that this individual is incompetent. He fell down three storeys, oblivious to the guard rail!! He is clumsy and careless, oblivious to limits, and gets himself in terrible predicaments. (Now really we should be thinking about inadequate supervision. How could somebody leave a child alone in this dangerous environment? And given this, we will understand that Steve may rightly distrust authority figures who have not come through for him, at least in that circumstance. But remember, the subconscious is going to conclude that if he had this experience exploring an environment and wound up falling 3 storeys, at the end of the day he can not trust *himself* to move forward in the world. And that belief is a recipe for disaster!).

So we see the themes of memory one and memory two: On one hand, he is fearful. On the other hand, he knows himself to be incompetent. In either case, he has every reason to be afraid! He can look forward to a life of injuries and hospital visits!

What's the solution? The third memory suggests that he should therefore preoccupy himself with thinking and wondering and reflecting. In memory three, he's pointing to the cleft chin. He's noticing. He's talking. That's where the perfectionism comes into this. He notices, he talks, he thinks, and he avoids activating; we speculate he fears any time he activates, he will either fail, fall or otherwise hurt himself!

The third memory also has him focusing, noticing, prioritizing looks. He himself also happens to have a cleft chin! The focus would be to emphasize the visual, how he looks, posturing, getting noticed for his good looks, acting 'as if'. And that was how he conducted himself in relationship and elsewhere! An actor, par excellence! I started to guess that his drug use had him medicating a baseline degree of anxiety, all relating to doubts about his own competence! All this going on well out of his conscious awareness!

Now it's quite ironic. Here is a guy who is extremely athletic, physically fit, huge muscles. His look is that of the prototypical handsome masculine man. And he was good at his job! But we see that the subconscious can easily harbour a map that stands in direct conflict to the perceptions that others have of him. The reality was that he was very functional. But the subconscious speculated otherwise, perceiving himself to be dangerously incompetent! Look at the memories! Who is competent in these memories? The doctors and the nurses. Certainly not him. The most he can do is call out for help if he sees ghosts. In his memories, others are the initiators. He is the recipient of their actions, for better, or, other times, for worse.

Let's move along to the next memories:

> 4. Nap time at kindergarten
> Vivid moment: seeing other children lying down
> Vivid feeling: contentment

The next memory takes things in the next logical direction. If he's not good at doing things, he should just spend time lying down. Nap time at school! Now that's what he's currently doing with any number of women! He gives himself permission to lie down quite a bit because when he lies down he is not at risk of, say, falling down three storeys! The subconscious tells him, "don't try to do things! It could be dangerous!"

> 5. Losing my balloons after carnival
> Vivid moment: watching them drift to the sky
> Vivid feeling: anger, pain

See that! Not only can he not dynamically move into the environment with an intention to do something, explore, etc, but even if he tries to retain what he has, so pathetic is he, he will not succeed. In this world, we have to accomplish things. We have to move and do. But his subconscious is so convinced that any time he does something he's really going to mess it up and there will be terrible ramifications. Imagine all the anxiety he would have associated with the obvious need to be competent at work and elsewhere.

> 6. Being sexually abused by best friend
> Vivid moment: storage locker, under bed
> Vivid feeling: confusion

The next memory probably gets us to the heart of the problem. In that experience, he probably felt 'done to' and likely the experience deprived him of growing into his sexuality and his masculinity at the right time, in the right way. Note that the person who did it was his best friend. Hence the trust issues. Now see that the map tells him that people who you are really close to will betray you. Subsequently, understandably, he will betray people with whom he is close. Of course! That's what the early memories/map says!

> 7. Grade 1, student throwing rock in my ear
> Vivid moment: my teacher trying to get it out
> Vivid feeling: embarrassment

In the next memory, again he is a recipient of others actions. Others are dominant. Others are the doers. He is never the hero, the masculine one. He is in an awkward *Yin* role (as in *Yin* and *Yang*, the primal feminine and masculine, which will be further discussed in the next chapter), whether because the doctors have to treat him, the friend abuses him or the student throws a rock that lodges in his ear.

And so with him we see a struggle with masculinity. No wonder he is so promiscuous. He constantly has to prove his masculinity.

When I told him that he was struggling with his masculinity and harbored terrible doubt about it, initially he thought I was crazy! He told me in no uncertain terms, "I do NOT have a problem with my masculinity." But then we went through the projective material including the memories and he could see it clearly for himself. He cried. It was so ironic. He was physically so strong and athletic. Why should he have these doubts about himself?

> 8. Telling my mother a policeman let me play with gun
> Vivid moment: mom's disbelief
> Vivid feeling: astonishment

Look at the next memory: 'telling my mother a police man let me play with his gun'. He knows he's lying. But what does a little boy want? He wants to be masculine. So in this memory the subconscious tells him that though he wants to be the big man, the closest he can come is 'acting as if'- lying about it. Even then nobody will believe him. How frustrating!

> 9. Neighbors in building being robbed
> Vivid moment: footprints in back driveway
> Vivid feeling: uneasy excitement

Next memory: The excitement of seeing the footprints of those who stole. I explained to him that masculinity involves harnessing masculine strength and using it to build something constructive. For he who perceives himself as weak and vulnerable, believing his masculine charge is paltry, the next best thing is becoming a rebel, being defiant. Rebellion is a hollow expression of power. For a few minutes, you feel like the man! But what have you built, really? You have nothing to show for it! Except that you pulled something off, you stole something. Where is the life satisfaction in that?

> 10. Halloween party at first public school
> vivid moment: the haunted house
> vivid feeling: total fear

And the last memory takes us back to the first of the series: fear. This guy experiences anxiety and self-doubt, as a person necessarily would if the masculine drive is blocked or poorly developed. He has the active imagination of a child, because, on a certain level, he is a child, lacking the toughness we get from what Chinese medicine would call the *Yang*, or masculine impulse. He subsequently squanders his masculinity and that does him no good. This fellow was stuck, as indicated by 10 memories that start with fear and end with fear. The system is sealed. He had been playing out this narrative for decades. This was the same map he had been using from age 5? 6? It was time for an upgrade![1]

What Happened Next . . .

Reviewing the memories and other projective material he had submitted, gave Steve the opportunity to see his map and to see 'where he was aiming'. It was powerful feedback. It was painful to think that at his age (30's), some men had built businesses, accumulated wealth, started families. What did he have to show? He could see the root issue: doubt about masculinity and an unproductive pattern that had him expressing sexuality in a counterproductive way, all to prove himself masculine.

He left our session, understanding that I was recommending treatment for drug addiction. I didn't expect to hear from him again. But three weeks later, in a rather bold gesture, he left an envelope under the office door, with a cheque for money he owed and a short message: "I will call you Monday to set up our first appointment."

Hmmm. Maybe he didn't understand me, I thought. We spoke on the phone. He had stopped using cocaine. He insisted that we do some work. He pressed. I agreed.

We met 10 times. We worked specifically on building his perception of himself as strong and dynamic. We changed the map! For the next 10 years, I received a New Year's card every January from Steve with pictures of the sons he had in the aftermath of our work together. He gave up the drugs, quit cigarettes and became a very active and devoted dad. His initial problem was with the hero archetype. He needed to revise an outdated map that had been put together at a very young age and remained ensconced in his adaptive unconscious.

Steve's New Map

The interesting thing about the Earliest Recollection Test is that changes in the life map will show up if you administer the test again. Case in point. After 10 sessions, I had Steve once again compile his 10 earliest memories. The directions are the same and, when I am administering the test a second time, I ask my clients not to reread the memories they wrote down the first time. Sometimes some or all of the memories they come up with will be the same. Even if they are the same, they may be remembered differently, reflecting some changes. Or, as in the case of Steve, the memories can be totally different.

You will note that the memories that Steve generated were those of an age that had him older, likely a function of the fact that he had shifted to a more mature consciousness; he felt more capable and more mature. As a rule, I analyse whatever people submit. Regardless of the age of the subject in the memories, we will trace the themes that come up and see what shifts, if any, we can notice.

Read those 10 memories and jot down some notes. How would you interpret these memories? Do you see any patterns here? Of course, we will be comparing the map that we read here to his earlier map. Let's see what we notice.

Steve's Next Set of Memories

1) Winning the coveted Scout of the Year award.

2) The excitement I felt when in 1973, my family moved out East. My first day there was a beautiful June day. My home was located on the hilltop overlooking a basin. An adventurous walk led me to a vacant lot with a clear view of the entire basin. I was in my glory, as on that day the Navy was maneuvering before my very eyes. A dozen or so destroyers, supply ships and submarines were involved. Providing me with a great display to welcome me to my new province.

3) On vacation in southern Ontario for two weeks in the summer, the most important stop along the way was at my uncle's. My uncle had a John Deere tractor/mower that he would let my brother and I ride. This machine did not exceed 7 miles an hour. Didn't matter. It might as well have been Space Mountain at Disney World!

4) The weird difference that I felt in high school when I was publicly recognized for being a member of both the ski team and the golfing team in the same year. How I came to be proud of the ski team and embarrassed of the golf team, I don't know. So completely embarrassed,

in fact, I skipped the second round of the golf tournament because I was too embarrassed to leave the school with my golf clubs.

5) A slow family walk up the highest of the Gatineau Hills outside of our neighborhood in Ottawa. Although physically tiring for a boy, it was always an interesting day of learning. For two years in a row, watching the same family of beavers building their dams in the spring.

6) My mother's pineapple upside down cake! Nuff said!

7) My very first job. A Toronto Star paperboy. An ambitious route that included over 90 Saturday Star deliveries. It was a seven day a week job/ delivery Monday to Friday, and most of my Sundays spent collecting. I purchased my first stereo set at sellers for $100 with the money I earned. It provided me a few years of private listening enjoyment.

8) Always in for some trouble prone excitement, my friends and I strung dozens of heavy duty elastic bands together. We agreed that the best use for this contraption was to hide in my friend's front yard bush and stretch as far back as possible, release, and with a resounding "thwack," get the first unsuspecting car that happened by. Only moments of pre-teenage fun to be had. As on the third or fourth attempt our device no sooner caught the bumper of a bus and was carried away.

9) Getting free chocolate milk from the milkman. I wonder if he was a perv. ha ha.

10) From 1997 to 1980 my love for the television show Star Trek grew to momentous proportion. There were two viewings a day. I would even take notes. To this day, I can tell you whatever he shows title is and proudly can recite dialogue, word for word, with the show.

Your thoughts?

Interpretation of Second Set of Memories

We are going to look at these memories using the same frame that we talked about initially. Look at the first three memories to see two different sides of an issue revealed in the first and second memory, with the third memory reconciling the earlier ideas.

> 1) Winning the coveted Scout of the Year award.
>
> 2) The excitement I felt when in 1973, my family moved out East. My first day there was a beautiful June day. My home was located on the hilltop overlooking a basin. An adventurous walk led me to a vacant lot with a clear view of the entire basin. I was in my glory, as on that day the Navy was maneuvering before my very eyes. A dozen or so destroyers, supply ships and submarines were involved. Providing me with a great display to welcome me to my new province.
>
> 3) On vacation for two weeks in the summer, the most important stop along the way was at my uncles. My uncle had a John Deere tractor/mower that he would let my brother and I ride. This machine did not exceed 7 miles an hour. Didn't matter. It might as well have been space Mountain at Disney World!

Notice three messages that specifically relate to masculinity. The first memory reveals the idea that Steve was/is recognized for his competence and so his competence is objectively established. The second memory shows this magnificent display of masculinity in the world at large, naval ships maneuvering, changing their positions. He looks from above. I interpret this memory as a metaphor or symbol. As an aside, I will often interpret memories symbolically. In this case I see this memory as the subconscious indicating symbolically that there has been a very dramatic awakening of masculinity *within*. The memory symbolically represents a process that is unfolding internally: the masculinity is awakened, and stands in formation, shifting, activating . . .

The third memory brings those two together: others see his competence and he can feel an awakening of his masculinity, as if he has arrived on his first day in a new place to call home (adulthood!). The third memory has him in a distinctly masculine moment: riding the tractor! Thrusting forward! Associating to the masculine experience of forward movement. Dynamism! Mastery!

Now it's interesting. Steve was always athletic. He played many sports. Only now, when he was making personal changes, could he access memories and associations to his physical strength and masculinity. Note how dramatically the map has changed and continues to change. But remember, change occurs gradually. People don't go from feeling weak and disempowered to the opposite, overnight. The shift is gradual.

> 4) The weird difference that I felt in high school when I was publicly recognized for being a member of both the ski team and the golfing team in the same year. How I came to be proud of the ski team and embarrassed of the golf team, I don't know. So completely embarrassed, in fact, I skipped the second round of the golf tournament because I was too embarrassed to leave the school with my golf clubs.

Look at memory number four. The pride being on the ski team and the shame being on the golf team. Initially his self-concept was steeped in doubt and negativity. Now he is moving to a position of positivity. The first three memories are extremely positive. The fourth one is partly positive and partly negative. We expect that over time he will move fully to a fully positive self-concept. Now he is in transition, half there, half in the old place.

> 5) A slow family walk up the highest of the Gatineau Hills outside of our neighborhood in Ottawa. Although physically tiring for a boy, it was

always an interesting day of learning. For two years in a row, watching the same family of beavers building their dams in the spring.

The fifth memory is extremely important. He's associated to a moment of dynamism, hiking with his family. But what is notable here? The beavers building the dam. In other words, one of the focal points of our work was to show that self-restraint, placing dams – around sexuality, I interpret – sublimates that energy in a productive way, a goal for the healthy male which then makes way for family life. A beautiful metaphor, a beautiful learning. At the time he wrote this, his partner had become pregnant, though they had not been trying to conceive. He was extremely excited, and ultimately transitioned nicely to the role of father.

6) My mother's pineapple upside down cake! Nuff said!

I would suggest that the interpretation of the sixth memory is the concept of reversal, something turning into its opposite. Indeed, he moved from the philandering boyfriend to the devoted father. He would intermittently call me to tell me about landmark moments: the birth of his sons; the fact that he quit smoking after decades of dealing with that addiction. He truly turned his life around. How delicious is that!

7) My very first job. A Toronto Star paperboy. An ambitious route that included over 90 Saturday Star deliveries. It was a seven day a week job/ delivery Monday to Friday, and most of my Sundays spent collecting. I purchased my first stereo set at sellers for $100 with the money I earned. It provided me a few years of private listening enjoyment.

8) Always in for some trouble prone excitement, my friends and I strung dozens of heavy duty elastic bands together. We agreed that the best use for this contraption was to hide in my friend's front yard bush and

stretch as far back as possible, release, and with a resounding "thwack," get the first unsuspecting car that happened by. Only moments of pre-teenage fun to be had. As on the third or fourth attempt our device no sooner caught the bumper of a bus and was carried away.

The next two memories are distinctly masculine: remembering the first job and remembering a moment of troublemaking with the guys. In each case, the masculine theme of thrusting; delivering a paper route, shooting elastics at cars. But in the rebellious second memory there the so-called delinquent behavior is short-lived. The elastic disappears. The incident is over. In these memories we have the representation of a first day in a new place, a first job. The energy is of turning a new leaf and so the recollection of untoward behavior is brief and passing. Something that will float into the past and be gone.

9) Getting free chocolate milk from the milkman. I wonder if he was a perv. ha ha.

The ninth memory we have the chocolate milk. Steve really enjoyed his fun, and so we still have an expression of pleasure seeking. Still a hint of sexual impropriety. Last time around, though, he was sexually abused. This time around we just have a speculation about improper, unwholesome intentions. The stain of sexual misconduct is getting lighter.

10) From 1997 to 1980 my love for the television show Star Trek grew to momentous proportion. There were two viewings a day. I would even take notes. To this day, I can tell you whatever the shows title is and proudly can recite dialogue, word for word, with the show.

The 10th memory is very important. We learn of a very important capacity. He is showing his capacity to be a disciple, to sit at the foot of the sage, a really important archetype. Sadly I often get memories of clients sitting avidly at the foot of the TV, and in this case the sage is the TV! But Steve's dedication to Star Trek (a decidedly masculine show, I might add), his effort to learn the lines, would be something that was directly relevant in the work I ultimately did with him.

When we started the therapy, we built on one particular moment in his life that occurred years earlier. About 10 years prior he had gotten Tony Robbins tapes and listened every day for six weeks; he successfully quit smoking for that six week period. After that, he began smoking again. But it didn't matter. Because we had a resource memory. He had already proven that he could, so to speak, sit at the knee of the sage and take instruction, follow directions and make changes. We built on that in the therapy.

Once this capacity to yield to the sage is part of his working identity. He knows this about himself forevermore. He will be able to take on more and will find the discipline to achieve. Because he knows that he can derive nourishment by assuming the role of disciple, the world will present him with role models and father figures. Remember . . . "when the student is ready, the teacher appears."

Did you notice we had no memories of father in either series? Makes sense, right? So the therapy had to help him cultivate *Yang*, a consciousness of the healthy fatherly perspective, and ultimately lead to his successful transition into fatherhood.

Now one could argue that the changes reflected in the second set of memories were contrived, a function of the recency effect given our sessions designed to shift his consciousness to that of an older, more mature and confident person. If that is the case, that is exactly what therapy is supposed to achieve! As a therapist, I want old long-forgotten memories of mastery to come to mind! So whether his choice of memories was driven by the therapy or reflective of unconscious internal shifts is not that relevant. That which we work to consciously change today, will become second nature tomorrow, as the new identity gradually settles in and becomes the new normal. 2

What about Your Memories?

Now that we have reviewed two sets of early memories, you might scan yours. Can you follow a narrative? Imagine each memory was a lesson. How does it follow from the last memory/lesson? What does each new memory add to the narrative? See if you can come up with the thread that connects them all.

Consider asking your friend to give you his or her 10 early memories. Then try this process using memories that are not your own. It's possible that it's easier to find that thread, at least initially, when you are dealing with somebody else's memories. We have less of a blind spot when we are dealing with the narrative of somebody else! Analyzing someone else's memories first gets you into the hang of it.

As well, see if you can interest a few friends in the project of learning about memories. If you all write out your memories, then you can take them up collectively. Let people who know you help you find the logic that explains the sequence and content of your memories. See if some themes become obvious.

Notes

1. As a side note, if you want to get a feel what the person's map is relative to romantic relationship, check out the 10 memories. Only a few of

these memories have him interacting with others, and of those, only one has him relating to a female, his mother. What is he doing in that memory? Lying! That's his map! He doesn't have a sophisticated map for relating to women so his map has him lying, acting 'as if' until he gets found out, which is inevitable!

2. Another way that new identity takes root, as an aside, is cognitively. The individual in a process of change begins to notice new thoughts that pop to mind, thoughts born of confidence. Carl Whitaker, a prominent psychiatrist, used to say, "Listen for the baby thoughts!" Clients can watch as they intermittently notice thoughts that are different than the usual, thoughts that reflect a change in self-image, a new attitude.

9

Interpreting Memories by Finding Patterns

"The magic behind magic is pattern."

Douglas Hofstadter

In the last chapter we looked at a sequence of 10 memories, considering how memories implicitly relay information, thereby forwarding an unspoken narrative. Each memory advances ideas, building on those ideas expressed by other memories in the sequence. Can we uncover a rationale that would account for how and why each memory leads to the next?

In this chapter, we look at patterns. Looking at 10 memories, you expect to find many themes represented in the various memories indicating a range of lessons the individual has accumulated about many disparate aspects of life. But often you will see one pattern shows up again and again in the various memories. In the last chapter, the first set of Steve's memories showed a recurrent theme: disempowerment. Instead of 'can do' we saw, 'can't do'. Wherever you find repetition, you are finding a deeply embedded belief that goes way back. Looking for patterns will help you identify rigid beliefs, idiosyncrasies, dominant character traits or anything that is pronounced in the personality. What follows next are a few themes to consider when you look at sets of memories.

Before we dive in, I must mention that while the technique of analyzing memories was initially developed by Alfred Adler, his students and followers more fully developed the method over years of use and study. The most influential texts that informed my skill acquisition were those by Shulman & Mosak (1988) and Powers & Griffith (1987). Many of the ideas I summarize derive from my study of Adlerian psychology, other areas of study in the domain of psychology, and these classic texts that are seminal in the field. Readers are encouraged to consult these texts for a far more comprehensive treatment of how memories are analyzed. Here I have prepared an introduction for the layman. I should also mention, in the pages that follow, I am also presenting some other angles which I have found useful in my clinical practice over the last 25 years.

Yin and *Yang*

If you are familiar with Eastern culture, you may know the ancient *Taiji* symbol. Let's review the meaning of that symbol to access an insight regarding psychological health that will help us analyze memories.

The Chinese refer to the way the universe functions as the *Tao*. Out of the unity of the *Tao*, the duality of the world emerges, referred to as *Yin* and *Yang*. *Yin-Yang* represents the polar nature of the world. Time is divided into day and night and literally every continuum has two opposite poles: hot and cold, active and passive, wet and dry, etc.

Even the processes of the world are characterized by this duality. Sound waves or light waves oscillate. Each wave has a peak and a trough. The body has countless rhythms characterized by the *Yin Yang* cycle. In respiration, there is the inhalation and the release; the heart fills, and then pumps the blood; peristalsis is characterized by a similar two part cycle. The two polar opposites create a unified balance in the body and the personality, as well. *Yang* is active during the day, but *Yin* becomes the guide when a moment requires submission to authority or the humility to ask for help. *Yin* is operative at night when we sleep but when we inaugurate activity, we activate with the help of *Yang*.

We expect to see both polarities reflected in the 10 memories because they both are the stuff of life. If you review Steve's first memories, his initial map of meaning, you see the dominance of *Yin*, albeit not in a particularly healthy manifestation; he experiences himself as done to and does not identify with the hero archetype, the 'can do' mentality. By the second memories, we see the healthy emergence of *Yang*.

When looking at a set of memories, if every memory has the *Yang* quality in which the person is active and dynamic, you are observing a theme of control. This is the person who, full of energy, likes to be active and dominant. Such a person may need to amplify and master the *Yin* dimension of life, which gives a person the ability to be submissive when that behaviour is appropriate. Sometimes we rightly need to surrender control and allow other people to take over.

If the memories are too *Yin*, there may be many memories watching others be dynamic, or you may see many silent memories. Vision is a passive sense. Memories that are too *Yin*, so to speak, may indicate the other side of imbalance. Such a person may need to cultivate a stronger association to their own competence and ability. Ideally, we hope to see balance in the memories, some *Yin,* some *Yang*.

Perceptual Style

Related to the above, people often have one more dominant sense which may be revealed in the memories. The highly visual individual may have memories which imprint seeing something that makes a strong impression. Often in these memories the person recalls a moment in which he or she is passive. The visual sense is one of beholding. Nothing is required. These are often silent memories; no one is talking. This pattern in memories may suggest that auditory processing skills are weaker, resulting in shyness or anxiety in social situations.

Another individual may have a stronger auditory orientation. Speech is more important in the memories, whether talking or listening. In that case, memories may show more emphasis on interaction with others. Are there also memories which depict physical doing? If not, the memories could indicate someone who needs to become more embodied, more kinesthetic, more associated to functioning physically. Time to get out more!

Some people are more dominant with regards to the kinesthetic sense, their memories may depict experiences where they were physically doing something. As mentioned in the *Yang* personality, control is an issue.

As always, our goal is to cultivate balance. If a set of memories never represent the individual speaking we are alerted to a person who needs to find his or her voice. Assertiveness training, singing lessons, journaling can all be helpful here. The auditory channel needs tweaking.

To many memories showing the person as physically passive? Such a person needs to build a perception of self as dynamic doer! Recommend the gym, taking up a sport, enrolling in comedy improvisation classes! Get moving!

If the memories are mostly about kinesthetic doing, this individual may be out of touch with some of the subtle norms that govern social interaction. These can be the memories of the one who talks over others and is overbearing. For real interaction, there is a give-and-take. Sometimes a person needs to listen! Advise the bearer of these memories to activate more *Yin:* less talking, more listening!

What's Your Name?

Here's another trick. Look up your first name on the Internet to find out what your name means. Why? The Talmud teaches that one of the only sources of prophecy that exists today is when parents name their children. According to this teaching, parents have an intuitive grasp, completely subconscious, of the essence of their child and they pick a name that will represent that essence. With every client, I always ask about the meaning of first and middle names. A person's life mission, their gift, and even their challenge, may be represented in that name.

Maybe you go onto the web and search the meaning of your name and the meaning doesn't speak to you. If that happens, you may be inclined to reject the idea that that name is, in fact, relevant; you are just not connecting the dots. It's hard for me to fully demonstrate the relevance of people's names in a publication like this. Firstly, the need to maintain confidentiality prevents me from sharing the names of clients who allowed their materials to be published. Secondly, my clinical practice goes well beyond analyzing memories. To do assessments, I analyze stories and drawings I have clients produce, I analyze handwriting and I administer other tests and interpret the findings, all within one all-encompassing assessment. Interpreting the name in the context of an intensive 'look under the hood' brings out nuances and meanings that relate to the breadth of what emerges. It is beyond the scope of this book to present an exhaustive look at any one individual. I, therefore, ask readers to take my claim about the meaning of names and their relevance to a person's essence on faith.

In the case of Steve (not his real name) in the last chapter, his actual name connotes strength and truth. So there he was, immersed in a life of lies motored by his belief that he lacked masculine strength. Often, our essential virtue is buried beneath the veneer of the opposite vice; we then have to fight to become who we are meant to be. Your name may provide clues and once you find that meaning, look over those memories again. See if a relevant theme emerges.

Movement

As you recall, Jordan Peterson teaches us that life is all about action. So don't be surprised when Adlerians make the same point. Powers and Griffith (1987) suggest that memories should be analyzed to notice who in the memory moves, in what way, in which direction and towards what impact. The memories show you how you are prepared to move and how you expect others to move.

Look at the memories. Who in the memories are effective? Teachers? Adults? Parents? Self? Friends? Who is not effective? As soon as you see any pattern, you are seeing a generalization. If every time a teacher in a memory is being mean, you are seeing a generalization about authority figures.

Look at the extent of participation and cooperation. Is the person with others or alone? If others appear in the memory, are they relating with the person whose memory you are analyzing? What is the person's role in the memory: a leader, a follower, a rebel, a victim? Is the person on the receiving end of others' actions or are others beneficiaries of their actions? Or is the person disengaged from others?

Look at gender in the memories. Are members of only one sex represented? Is one sex represented as superior or dominant over the other sex? Are stories related of good men and bad women? Or vice versa? If the memories are submitted by a heterosexual female, reviewing all the memories will show you how she relates to members of the opposite gender. If memories depict that boys and men are supportive, she will likely find a partner with the same qualities. Antagonistic? Distant? That's what she will find, as per the Carrie Fisher memory described in an earlier chapter.

As you see in the map, that is what you will find in the life! Those memories show the DNA which will play out in future relationships over time. That's one good reason why a person might want to work on changing the map! Especially if the relationship that was modeled via parents was problematic.

Content

Do you see a certain subject matter come up again and again in the memories? Play? Work? Sexuality? When the same theme emerges several times, we are alerted to an area that is an emphasis, or perhaps a preoccupation. Also look for what we rightly expect to find in terms of content. You would think that some of the memories will happen in the home environment. How is the home represented? If there are no memories at home, what was going on at home that there are no such memories? We expect some memories of parents. Are they represented in the memories? Only one? Wonder about that.

When we did not see Steve's father in any of the memories in the last chapter we guessed the problem we saw partly related to him lacking a role model. We also saw that he did not have adequate supervision. Where was father? There was a lack of protection in his early years. No wonder he got into trouble.

Are peers represented in the memories? If not, it's good to get some additional memories so we can get a feeling for those relationships. If most of the memories feature adults, it may reflect a person who always interacted with authority figures at the expense of socializing with others the same age.

Positive or Negative

Is there a pattern where memories are either consistently positive or consistently negative. If each memory recounts an amazing moment where something spectacular happened, you have to consider that this is a sign of 'all or nothing' tendencies. This may indicate a person who loves when things are larger-than-life but has a very low threshold for that which is boring, average or even the inevitable negative moments that punctuate life. If the memories are consistently negative, we may be seeing the glass half empty phenomena and it may relate to trauma or difficulties in the past that have not been effectively processed.

Archetypes

Keep your eyes open for archetypes. Archetypes are psychological patterns. The hero, the mother, the father, the wise elder, the teacher, are all archetypes, bigger than any one individual who plays that role in our lives. We will often find that we struggle with one archetype or another. If there was a difficult relationship with mother, the mother archetype is loaded. There may be conflict with mother figures or a desperate drive to attract mothering from others. Mastering the role of mother might be incredibly important for such a person.

We may have struggles with certain archetypes or attractions to others. One person may be called to wisdom and driven to seek out learned people. In this day and age, some of the archetypes are represented by celebrities. The Fool, the Princess, the Queen, the list goes on and on. Through the memories you may see pronounced interest in one archetype or another, or evidence that there was a deficiency with regards to an archetype. Keep your eyes open for that.

In Steve's 10 memories, we saw missing authority figures, conspicuous by their absence at certain moments in his life when they would have come in handy. And we saw a missing father. On the other hand the archetype of the rebel was very obvious: the robbers, lying to the police officer, a friend sexually abusing him and even his own initial behaviour: defying the restraining panels on the third floor porch, resulting in a serious accident. The archetype of the rebel was an important part of his initial map of meaning, though not particularly useful with regards to creating a life with purpose. Strengthening the archetype of the hero was part of the remedy that would grow his masculine identity.

Typology

Another tool that can help you out when looking at your memories, is a really interesting typology system developed by Sally Hogshead. Visit www.howtofascinate.com and take her free test to figure out your more dominant trait, then check out her book, *How the World Sees You* so you can figure out your specific 'type' according to her model. Her system identifies 49 different personality types, centered around 7 primary and secondary personality traits. I find her system to be accurate.

Usually you will see how your 10 memories also encode something about your unique life task. If you discover you are a 'defender' or 'change agent' or one of her other types, you may notice that the themes she describes actually come through in your 10 memories! Working with her system is a bit like a cheat sheet! It let's you articulate some patterns which then, once you are alert to them, might help you see that the themes that shine through in the 10 memories!

There are other typologies you can use. I find many of these systems to be useful and interesting. This one is a good starting point, though. And if you explored others – MBTI types, Enneagram or others, look at your memories through the lens of that model and see if the type that seems relevant comes through in your memories.

On Self-Compassion

Peterson's work teaches us that we must move from chaos to order. Bear in mind that in our lives, we ultimately need to landscape the unconscious terrain, which is always a more chaotic, primal and less ordered version of self. The fact that it integrated flawed concepts when you were at an age when you could do no better is no fault of your own. Just as the earth, in Genesis, is described, initially as chaotic, with the Divine spirit hovering over the deep (not infusing the deep below, but quite seperate from it – no wonder there is chaos!) so, too, we initially are in our more chaotic form. By undertaking an ordering process, we can take ourselves to higher levels. Steve's first memories, the first incarnation, were primitive – uninformed – the second, inspired, possessing clarity and positivity. We start chaotic, and with a little effort, we add order and organization, shaping ourselves into the hero that reflects our best self. That's what Steve did. It's another form of "cleaning your room!"

Sarah Yehudit Schneider, a teacher of Jewish Mysticism in Jerusalem, uses the metaphor of a puzzle to describe the life task of perfecting the self. She suggests that each person is like a puzzle piece designed to fit in with all the other pieces/souls. The task is to find your own "contours, the right curves and grooves" so as to properly fit. In order for things to work out, everybody must do their work, properly bringing out their edges in a way that represents their best destiny. We are helped by what she terms "the breath of the bones," an intuitive program locked within that guides us towards our best future. Our task is to listen carefully for "the still small voice" within which carries the message that will guide us forward. Schneider's teachings, in fact, are offered under the auspices of thestillsmallvoice.org. Accessing that subtle message of destiny is work. Succeeding can take a lifetime. We need to be patient with ourselves. If it were a less lofty task, it would be easy and straightforward.

Interpreting Memories

When you are trying to get the hang of interpreting memories, the idea is to practice. It is tricky. Sometimes you can really puzzle over a series of memories. The person who submitted the memories, may, themselves, have insights that help you get to the right interpretation. Each series of memories you try to analyze will help hone the skill. Remember, this task is like learning a new language, that being the language of the subconscious. So in the next chapter, let's take on another set of 10 memories. More practice! Then take another crack at analyzing your own memories. And if you feel stuck and still struggle to figure out what those memories of yours are telling you, the book in the Recommended Reading section explains the process in great detail. Or you can consult an Adlerian therapist in your vicinity who can shine light on what you might be missing!

10

"Analyze That!" Karen's Memories

Karen came in for an assessment as a 30 something project manager seeking clarity and direction. She had a history of mental health difficulties but, at this age, was functioning well, though ambivalent about her work. She had a somewhat volatile relationship with her boyfriend who had mental health issues. Overall, she felt ripe for feedback, curious about next steps in her life and found the projective assessment process to be intriguing. I'm presenting Karen's 10 earliest memories here to further demonstrate how we analyze these memories.

Steve, in the last chapter, was quite clipped and abbreviated in how he executed the task of recording his memories. Karen did the opposite. Her memories were quite detailed and they will appear here slightly edited which will make them easier to work with.

Karen's Earliest Memories

1) I was about five years old and went on a day trip to a local lake with my best friend and her family and a few other friends of theirs. It was

the middle of a very hot summer. There was a long dock at the lake where we spent most of our time that day, jumping off into the water, swimming around to the ladder, back up and off the side of the dock again.

There was one point in the day, that we decided as a group that it would be fun to jump off the dock all at once. We had a plan – on the count of three, we'd all jump in. One – two – three! I jumped in. No one else did, I realized to my horror mid air. When I came back up to the surface all I could hear was laughter – the whole gang was pointing at me and laughing that they pulled one over on me. Not wanting to be a downer, I played along and laughed it off.

We decided to try again – for real this time. One, two, three! I couldn't believe they got me again. I was furious as I came back to the surface and scrambled back up onto the dock. This time I wasn't such a good sport and I made sure I would find a way to pull a prank on each of them the way they tricked me. Obviously knowing I would likely not be fooled a third time. One, two, three! They all jumped in the water as I stayed standing on the dock. They were all dying of laughter again as they surfaced and swam back to the dock. I was livid – my plan to not be fooled a third time had blown up in my face!

Now it was like a game of rock, paper, scissors – I was trying to figure out what move they would pull next. I tried a few more times to wriggle myself away from being the butt of everybody's joke. I think I finally managed to coordinate with them on the fifth jump in, feeling elated and proud of myself. Just in time for everyone to lose interest entirely in the game.

Vivid moment: seeing my best friend laugh at me alongside her family and other friends.

Vivid feeling: confused as to why she was in on and seemed to be delighting in the efforts to play a coordinated trick on me. Confused and frustrated by my confusion. I also then felt anger as a result, more so at myself in the end than the others for not being able to prevent them from making me repeatedly the butt of the joke.

2) I was about three or four years old and my mom had taken time off work to be with me before I started nursery school full time. My best friend lived right across the street and my mom would often watch over us both as we are essentially inseparable at the time. It was an early spring day in March, still lots of snow on the ground, and my mom had the idea to make a trip to a local conservation area – one of my absolute favorite places at the time – as a treat and then adventure for both of us. We packed a lunch of treats, too. We got to the conservation area and hunted around for any sign of wildlife – we came across some Canada geese – as it turned out to be an unseasonably warm and sunny day, full of activity. Our hike through the park lead to my favorite place – a jungle gym with an awesome slide, swings and seesaws. Bill and I climbed to the top of the slide after playing on the swings with our lunches and ate perched on the top of the slide like we were royals looking over our country.

Vivid moment: the taste of the honey and butter sandwiches. Eating them outside in the early spring air with my best friend beside me.

Vivid feeling: elation. I couldn't believe how many parts of that day aligned with my favorite things. I felt very lucky before understanding what that feeling was.

3) I was five years old and lying in my bed early one night. I'd likely been lying awake since my bedtime (as I regularly did) for a couple of hours. I heard the phone ring and my mom picked up, talking quietly before letting out a huge scream that terrified me. It took a few minutes to figure out whether she was crying and expressing joy or shock from bad news. I finally heard her tone shift back from aversion to joy and realize she had received very good news on the call. She hung up and I heard my parents talking to one another excitedly, before heading into my sister's room (who was still awake) and talking to her. They then

come into my room and told me they had exciting news. I sat up on the bed. The lights were still off.

"Were moving to Germany!" My mom exclaimed. They then proceeded to explain to me what this meant and why we were moving: mom applied for a teaching job with the Canadian military and she just found out she got the job. She was very happy because many people applied for the jobs but few got one. I felt I didn't fully understand what they were telling me and what it would mean but I knew I didn't like it. They would go without me because I wasn't leaving (I told them). They eventually softened me a bit to the idea that night by bribing me with German chocolate – as much as I could eat – when we arrived in our new home country.

Vivid moment: sitting up on the bed in the dark but for the light that came into the room from the hall

Vivid feeling: distrust – I didn't fully get what was happening and the implications but it was clearly bad news for me at the time.
(Note to reader: in the end, this woman did go to Germany with her family and it was an amazing life experience; she didn't want to leave when it was time to go!)

4) I was four years old and was visiting my grandparents while my sister, mom and dad were away on a ski trip. They lived in a small town at the time in the split-level bungalow style house on a quiet street near a ravine and by a nice big park. I loved visiting them. I was somewhat afraid of my grandmother because she was "stern" and could be icy at times. I was a little nervous going to visit and stay with them without the buffer of my parents.

To my surprise, Granny was warm, engaged and attentive. I was seeing a whole other side of her. We ate dinner the first night I was there in the lower level where the TV room was – watching wheel of fortune and then jeopardy while we ate. Later, the next day, Granny taught me how to use the organ in the TV room and my grandpa then sat and played some music for me. I felt like I had slipped seamlessly into their comfy life together and for those two days I felt like I was the most special kid – maybe their favorite grandchild? Ha!

Vivid moment: how comfortable I felt falling asleep upstairs the first night, leaving them downstairs with the soft murmur of late-night TV shows.

Vivid feeling: acceptance, love and attention. I couldn't believe I had ever been afraid of my granny even a little bit. I felt left out and upset at not being able to go on the trip with the rest of the family (I was too young to ski) but those feelings quickly vanished within hours of my stay at my grandparents.

5) I was five years old in the summer we moved to Germany. I knew we were leaving soon and things are going to change so it was a summer underscored by the tension of transition. I think as a result, I have many vivid memories from this period of time. My sister and I had started a tradition with my aunt who lived in Etobicoke of visiting her in the city in the summer for two packed days of girls' fun that included going to the movies, going shopping, visiting Wonderland and eating frosted flakes and Fruit Loops. I remember very vividly during this trip staying up past when my aunt and sister turned in and tiptoeing into the living room to peer out my aunt's west facing window to look at the lights of the city and the CN Tower. As a kid from a tiny rural town, I was transfixed. I felt in each light and the sparkling net of them all together a rush of endless possibility and the excitement of the unknown. I felt as though I could have stared out at the expanse of night skyline forever that night.

Vivid moment: standing at the window, feeling the rush of excitement in the plush living room carpet under my toes.

Vivid feeling: possibility and opportunity and feeling engaged, alert and alive.

6) I was five years old and it was halfway through our first year in Germany. Because my mom had the job, my dad was spending that year as a stay-at-home dad, taking care of me in the afternoons when I wasn't at school as Junior kindergarten was only half days. My dad would walk me to the bus stop every morning. I did catch the bus to school always sitting with my best friend at the time, Peter. On the bus ride home, Peter and I would get off at the same stop where his mom and my dad would be waiting to walk us each home.

This day Peter and I must've been deep in the chat because I remember finally looking out the bus window to see that we are no longer in town but driving out on a country road. I knew we had missed our stop so I walked up to the bus driver to ask where we were and I surprised him – he didn't know that there are any kids left on the bus. He seemed upset and started asking me where we lived. I told him the name of our town and he seemed to know which stop to take us back to in order to be picked up. When we finally got back to the stop, both of our parents were there looking quite weird. When we got off the bus, Peter's mom ran up and grabbed him, dragging him home and scolding him. My dad just rushed over and gave me a very tight hug which felt frantic. It scared me. I didn't fully understand why they both seemed so upset. We just took a little longer to get to our stop – of course it was far longer than I could appreciate, long enough for both of our parents to fear the worst.

Vivid moment: my dad's face and the tension and force in his hug when I got off the bus.

Vivid feeling: the sinking feeling of seeing our two parents at the bus stop and the transition from feeling happy-go-lucky on the bus to realizing something had gone wrong to make them both so upset.

7) I was about six and playing on the street outside of our apartment in the tiny village we lived in Germany with my sister, my dad and our close friend Grace who lived in the apartment below us. Something or

other my sister did pissed me off and we started squabbling. I crossed the line at some point and my dad told me to walk back to the house with him for a timeout. I was livid and fought him the whole way – how dare he make me miss any fun outside. Back at the apartment, I refuse to go in my room so he took me into my parents room for the timeout (carried me, kicking and screaming). I was so mad at him, I couldn't contain myself or get ahead of the rush of emotion. I was screaming at him, crying and begging him to let me rejoin the other two outside. He just sat quietly on his bed which made me even angrier.

In a quick moment, I noticed the open closet full of clothes and decided to grab them and throw them at my dad in protest. The first piece I grabbed was a windbreaker. I whipped it as hard as I could in my dad's direction. The jacket landed a bit short but in the process the zipper whipped him right in the eye. After recovering for a minute, he grabbed me and spanked me twice. It hurt like nothing I'd felt before. This was the first time my dad had ever spanked me.

Vivid moment: the moment I threw the jacket and realized I had hurt my dad. I was instantly overcome with regret, remorse for my actions and guilt.

Vivid feeling: regret in the moment I realized I'd gone too far and wasn't in control of my actions.

8) I was around six years old and was ecstatic that my aunt and uncle are not only visiting us in Germany (coming from Canada), but they were coming on a trip we booked with our very close friends, the Smiths, to Turkey over the March break. The day they arrived, my parents both had to work so they watched over us on a day off from school. My uncle, who can play piano by sight, came out in nothing but boxer shorts with hearts on them in the morning, which absolutely killed us with laughter, and spent the morning playing rock tunes for us as we danced and sang along with my aunt. My most vivid memory of the morning was us dancing and singing to his rendition of hound dog.

Vivid moment: my uncle slamming the keys and belting out singing in his booming voice, while sitting, playing piano in his heart boxers. I couldn't stop laughing.

Vivid feeling: absolute joy.

9) I was around six and my grandparents on my dad's side were visiting us for the first time in Germany. My grandparents were getting us ready for school as my parents were both off to work early and I was having trouble with the way my clothes were fitting (a very usual instance for me as a kid). Because we were running late to school, my sister and Granny were urging me to find something I like better, put it on and get going to the bus. Their efforts were in vain and I kept getting angrier and more frustrated with my clothes. Eventually my sister dragged me out the door which angered me even more so I stormed off ahead of her to the bus. To spite her for her actions, I dropped my backpack on the ground and kept walking. I knew she'd pick it out but hoped she wouldn't so I didn't have to continue to school. When I looked back, I saw my sister carrying my bag and my granny down the street, watching the scene from our apartment balcony.

Vivid moment: turning around to see my granny watching my fit on the street.

Vivid feeling: feeling both ashamed but very angry and not able to control my emotions or even get ahead of them.

10) I was about seven years old and I was over at my best friend Peter's house after school, where I would often go until my parents got home from work. I was incredibly hungry but too intimidated by Peter's mom to ask for a snack. I remember suggesting to him we go get something to eat in subtle ways, convincing him it was his idea and taking the pressure off me to ask, but he wasn't biting. Eventually he just asked me outright if I wanted a snack, to which I replied I would if he did but asked him to go to his mom asking for a snack for himself. I remember him walking out to the kitchen and telling his mom that I wanted a

snack but was too afraid to ask for myself. I could hear her say I needed to ask for myself and then she came into the room to tell me that. I hadn't felt that level of embarrassment before. I managed to squeak out that I was hungry but she just told me it was too close to their dinnertime to eat anything before. When she left, I wanted to start crying I was so embarrassed by how the scene unfolded. Peter's mom always intimidated me but I never fully bounced back around her after this scolding.

Vivid moment: hearing Peter's blunt and honest conversation with his mom, unable to stop him from what he was saying.

Vivid feeling: embarrassment to a level I had never experienced when his mom was scolding me for not speaking up.

> Okay, now you have read the 10 memories. If you are working on skill building, review the last chapter which gives you a structure for looking at the 10 memories, and then start to jot down notes as they relate to the various themes discussed in the last chapter. In the next chapter, we will interpret them together.

Notes

11

Interpreting Karen's Memories

In reviewing Karen's memories, let's start by considering the themes mentioned in the last chapter. Then, after we have looked at the memories from these perspectives, we can trace the sequence of the memories, and see how they advance a particular narrative. You can note that all names, including that of the client, have been changed, so we will not look at the meaning of her name lest that compromise Karen's privacy.

Yin and *Yang*

Looking from the perspective of life's great polarity which has us alternating between two states, dynamic and expressive versus receptive and internal, Karen demonstrates great range in her memories. In some memories, Karen engages dynamically, with intensity and complete abandon: throwing a fit in two memories and dancing and singing in another. In other memories, Karen is completely, sometimes deliciously, given over to the state of receptivity: so engaged in conversation with a friend she fails to register when it's time to get off the bus; her reverie looking out the window at her aunt's; a state of reflection and appreciation when at her grandparents'.

Yin and *Yang* are polar opposites and we must manifest and ultimately master the healthy experience of each. Here, though, we see extremes. Some moments depict her as having been dynamically engaged, jacked up with rage or given over in complete abandon when singing and dancing. At the other end of the spectrum, some memories had her enraptured, lost in a full experience of receptivity, enjoying companionship, the pleasures of eating, the reverie of the night sky. Her experiences in each case were fulsome and intense. She is somebody who can really appreciate and delight in the good in a given moment and really engage with others and with life.

The problem, though: we are seeing somebody who has difficulty calibrating. She runs hot and cold. If something is good, she marinates in it, she adores it, she thrives. But if something is less ideal, imperfect, she suffers, she is angry and unhappy. She will be prone to extremes in terms of her moods, a sign of emotional immaturity.

Now the first memory becomes easier to understand. Recall that the first memory makes an overriding statement about the life of the person. This memory is about confusion. "Do I go or do I stay?" *Yin* or *Yang*?

Time and time again she is going to be unclear about how to progress in life. In a moment where she should move forward, she will doubt. In a moment when she should throw on the brakes, she may accelerate. The subconscious tells her that she's really not very good at reading the room or reading contexts and when she makes a move she's often on the wrong side of progress. We expect she will therefore sit with a question about whether she can really trust herself and the decisions she makes. If she can't trust herself, it's going to be difficult to trust others. She may then find herself in situations with those who mustn't be trusted. (She was with her long term boyfriend who struggled with serious mental illness. She later discovered he was unfaithful. She was in a job where her hard work was exploited by those who could take credit. Historically, she made choices that took her off the path of where she rightly ought to go, leading to dead ends. She made important changes over the course of the therapy).

So in the memories, we see her moving to both ends of the continuum (which is good, and demonstrates flexibility and range) but in a way that lacks mastery. We prefer to see a memory where she delights in the chat that she is having with her friend Peter but instead of surrendering fully and wholly into the experience of *Yin* (associated with bonding and connecting) we want to see, in the same moment, that she has some mastery of purposeful *Yang*, which would have her well able to track where the bus is and competently track when she needs to get off. That would show her as a person who can deploy *Yang* in the midst of a *Yin* experience. Similarly, in the last memory she is hungry and shy (*Yin*) but we would wish to see healthy assertiveness (*Yang*) which would look like a full willingness to relay her message to the friend's mother and even insistence on getting the food she needs. That would show her activating *Yang* in a *Yin* context.

Looking from the perspective of *Yin* and *Yang*, we see some emotional immaturity and challenges with self-confidence that relate to the difficulty she has calibrating herself. We get a glimpse of the map of meaning and some insights into the kinds of changes and upgrades that would help her be more successful.

Perceptual Style

Based on the memories, let's call Karen gifted. Her auditory channel is dominant giving her excellent interpersonal skills and she therefore thrives in the realm of connecting with others, as seen in two memories showing her richly engaged in one on one conversation and singing with family members.

Another strong channel is the kinesthetic. Memories show her hiking, climbing, dancing, singing and swimming. Those who have a strong kinesthetic perceptual system tend to be more emotionally intense than those who are primarily of the auditory and/or visual style. She is 'embodied' and so emotions are powerfully embodied . . . taking full expression in experiencing rage and throwing fits; this is her history in childhood.

Note the first memory. The kids play this trick on her and she is very quick to trip into pride and anger. That's the kinesthetic type. They get flooded with anger and have more access to intensity than others would. After all, what's the big deal, you might say. But the kinesthetic type is very invested in doing and is more invested in winning and success than the other types. Her response to that event and her determination to "get them" is also consistent with the kinesthetic type.

We also see one memory that has her strongly visual, very engaged with what she sees out the window at her aunt's. We can tell her that she can use her visual sense to calm herself down when she feels upset. The subconscious shows us, in that memory, that the visual realm can be a source of relaxation.

Though the memories reveal that Karen needs to sort herself out a little bit, when we think about perceptual style, we see a person who is really going to go places in life. She is multifaceted and gifted. She is well-rounded in terms of her skill sets. When I gave her that feedback, she reflected that in school she was both good at sciences and good in the arts. She was told that most people excel at one or the other. She had both.

Movement

Central to this theme of movement is the fact that she is truly confused about how to move. Certainly we see it in the first memory when she is trying to decide whether to jump into the lake. But, really, she is often behaving in ways that are counter-intuitive. Look at the second memory. Why is she eating at the top of the slide? Other kids could come along to use the slide and there she will be with all her wrappers and all her food, needing to get out of everybody's way. In memory three, her mother screams in surprise and Karen freezes in shock. What's going on? It's a confusing moment. Memory 6 has her off task. She is lost in conversation with her friend when she should be watching for the bus stop so she won't miss her stop. In memories 7 and 9, she's throwing fits and will regret both incidences of rage later. In memory 10, she's being told by her friend to go and ask this mother for a snack and she tries to wiggle around fulfilling his directive. How often in these memories is she confused about the proper way to move forward?

Not surprisingly, she came in looking for feedback because she was confused. She was in the wrong relationship which became clear when she discovered the betrayal. She was at the wrong job. She awakened with great clarity to how she needed to move forward but in order to do this she needed to move out of the narrative characterized by confusion and self-doubt.

Content

Look deeper at these memories and you see one central problem: difficulty making transitions. In life, we come to a moment where we have to stop doing something and we have to start doing something else. Life constantly presents us with a beginning, a middle, and an end, and then we have to start at the next new beginning. My feedback to her was that this is where she struggles. Her distrust of herself was such that when it came to new beginnings she wasn't confident to take a step in any direction and so she would overstay and fail to take the next necessary step. In memory two, when she gets to the top of the slide, she's reached an end. The next thing she needs to do is a new beginning which involves going down the slide. She hedges. She waits. She avoids. And she ends up, in so doing, eating in a place where one rightly wouldn't normally set up to eat.

Mother announces the trip to Germany in memory three. But that involves a transition. So she knows immediately that she doesn't want to go because she doesn't like transitions. In reality, it was a wonderful adventure and she was very glad that she went. As soon as she hears about a transition, she gets nervous. In memory 4, we have another transition. She normally experiences her grandparents in a bit of a negative way and so she finds that when she actually goes there for the weekend she has a very pleasant experience. This is a good transition. Not only because she goes from her home environment to a weekend at a place where she has never stayed but also because she transits from one experience of her grandparents to a completely different and better experience. So here there is a lesson that sometimes even though you dread the transition, the experience is successful. She's beginning to show a change of heart about transitions as something to fear. But in memory 6, she fails the transition of getting off the bus at the right moment and fails the transition of moving from playing/following parental direction and going into the house for a time out, in memory 7. And of course memory 10 where she goes from playing to suddenly feeling hungry and needs to manage that in a successful way; that transition does not go well. So at root we find somebody who hedges whenever it's time to make a decision and move forward in a new and different way. This is where she falters.

Archetypes

In this series of memories, there are few memories which depict authority figures relating as such. We have memories where adults are almost in the role of peers: an uncle who sings and dances wearing only underwear, an aunt who isn't actually present in memory 5, grandparents who are downstairs at the point of the vivid moment in memory 4 (and she discovers they are not cranky and negative as she feared), mother is behaving like another sister, in memory 3, when she is getting exciting news and screaming like a teenager.

There is leadership in memory 7, in so far as father tries to implement the punishment but Karen does not bow to his authority. She rebels. In memory 9, when Karen throws a fit and tries to get out of going to school, her grandmother watches helplessly. In memory 10, Peter's mother appears to be an unkind and overly strict authority figure.

We conjecture that Karen does not take kindly to authority and has not cultivated a comfortable relationship with authority. We conjecture that this further fuels her doubt about her own decision-making ability. Where can she go for advice? Whose leadership does she follow? Has she cultivated her own authority? If not, she may have difficulty setting limits and be taken advantage of (which was happening at work).

In my work with Karen, I specifically wanted to help her cultivate a relationship with the archetype of the elder or the sage. I asked her to start listening to Jordan Peterson lectures. She began "binge" listening! This is somebody who has really needed to cultivate a healthy relationship with the archetype of the sage/teacher! The therapeutic relationship itself brings a client, ideally, into relationship with a teacher, as I would hope psychotherapists are teachers, guides and even elders. In the therapy, I additionally did specific work to help Karen warm to that archetype, to cultivate her interest in reading and learning, to help her connect to a source of inner wisdom within that more intuitively understood how she needed to move forward, upgrade her map and aim herself more productively. She left the boyfriend, left the job and decided to pursue a different career.

Typology

I had Karen take the questionnaire on Sally Hogshead's website (www.howtofascinate.com) and Karen strongly identified with the findings. The test determined that her two strongest traits were innovation and power. We certainly saw the power in her personality represented in those memories, fueling a strong temper and willfulness. We also see innovation in her memories. How often she is doing something off the beaten path. She is no slave to convention! She gives herself permission, at least as a child, to defy norms. And clearly she comes from a family where innovation is part of the family culture: uncle singing in his briefs and mother taking off to do a year sabbatical to teach overseas.

Sally Hogshead calls her type "The Change Agent," characterized by the following traits: inventive, untraditional and self-propelled. Karen strongly resonated with the profile that she received but we laughed about the fact that the Change Agent is somebody who easily traverses from one state to the next. I associate to a teaching of Stephen Wolinsky, a psychologist, who wrote, "in order to become who you truly are, first you have to become who you are not." That would seem to be true with regards to Karen. As a Change Agent, she would be one to spur others to change and one who would happily move towards change herself. So interesting that the first edition of her map of meaning showed her to be the exact opposite to what likely is her destiny and purpose on planet earth: to be she who masters transitions, and makes many of them!

Following the Sequence

Now we go back and look at the memories from the beginning. We imagine that the unconscious is providing a step-by-step communication which relays the map of meaning. Let's follow the sequence.

The first memory takes us to the concept that in life we often just have to jump in. We have to jump into the next thing that we are going to commit to. And there is this complexity in memory 1. It is as if the unconscious is saying, "you can't just jump in. There may be reason to hesitate. Don't jump!" So the first memory shows this reluctance to just "do it." Whereas the second memory shows her specifically not jumping in. There she is at the top of the slide. Normally one would just "jump." Go down the slide. So she camps out at the top there. She doesn't descend down. She starts but then stops the natural flow. There's always an interruption.

I didn't mention that she was doing her bachelor degree years earlier but took a moratorium in the middle because she was having mental health problems. If we probe, time and time again we will find that she just doesn't go from start to finish. There will be interruptions. She slows it down. There will often be a glitch.

Caroline Casey quips, "he who hesitates, gets bossed." So naturally, once she has established that she doesn't trust herself to descend and she halts instead, the third memory comes along to tell her that there will be times when change is imposed from without. That's the memory where she learns the family will move overseas. She immediately resists. She doesn't like these transitions. It catches her off guard. But, memory 4 reminds her that she had negative expectations about visiting her grandparents and look how nicely it worked out. Sometimes transitions are not as bad as she fears they will be. The map shows that she is having what we call "a change of heart." She is starting to think that maybe you can fear a negative outcome but then be pleasantly surprised. This occurs in memory 5. Though she's living in negative anticipation of the upcoming trip to Germany, she has a perfectly magical evening visiting her aunt. Clearly she is softening to the idea of change and transition.

But as soon as the last two memories start warming her to that which she has been resisting, more memories come which anchor her to her original reluctance. In memory 6 she misses her bus stop and it's as if the subconscious is telling her that transitions are hard to navigate and, maybe she's not good at it. She did, after all, miss her stop. Memory 7 gives another example of the same: she was supposed to leave the play area and listen to her father and she fought it tooth and nail. She responded badly, hurting her father and regretting it. Clearly, she's no good at making necessary transitions, even when she is given clear directives.

Memory 8 reminds her that she's good in environments where there is no need to make a transition. In that memory, she is thriving, enjoying the fun, playing the music and dancing, nowhere to go and nothing to do but be in the moment. These are ideal circumstances. Alas, life is rarely like that. Go to the next memory and it's that requisite moment of having to go to school (an unhappy transition) and she fights it tooth and nail. She ratifies what she knows: she's not one for making transitions.

But then memory 10 is problematic. It's one thing to avoid transitions because they are unpleasant but if she never becomes the master of making transitions then moments can come up which require her to be assertive and to get what she needs and here she is, "too shy to ask for a snack." Either she becomes the master of making transitions which will sometimes involve setting limits on herself but other times empower her to impose her will in the environment, or she will be at a disadvantage.

We can see from the memories themselves that she was already warming to the idea of making some important life changes and, of course, that's what drew her into psychotherapy to start with. When people are having a change of heart, the narrative of the memories appears to be in flux, almost arguing two sides of an idea. It's less work to incent people to make life changes when they are halfway there, having already started contemplating a new direction. In that case, these 'baby thoughts' will come through in the 10 memories. The map of meaning is undergoing a transition and upgrade!

From Chaos to Order

The 10 early memories can reveal the degree to which a person is struggling with chaos/immaturity having not yet cultivated order. We cultivate order through integrating the words, teachings and role modelling of teachers or authority figures (and sometimes via an intuitive felt sense). As a person progresses, dreams may represent the process of change, showing movement from chaos to order.

Shortly after the feedback session, Karen shared the following dream:

> I fell asleep outside and I turned into a painting of a person whose skin was the colors of the rainbow. I was curled up on the ground (in the painting so I was watching this objectively at the same time as it was happening to me subjectively) and then, from my body, roots sprouted and formed a tree, with my colorful body as the root system and trunk.

Becoming a painting, I would suggest, indicates the self-awareness that she gained upon getting feedback based on the memories and projective material. She could, as if, see herself as a person in the painting. And what she sees are all these colors of the rainbow, all the constituent parts of the personality but they are all present though not manifesting in an organized way that promotes function. She is curled up on the ground. She is not empowered. The dream starts with chaos.

And then she watches as the roots form and she becomes a tree with a trunk. Initially she is almost prostrate on the ground. But with this process that is organizing and empowering, a process that begins as she watches herself, she begins to flourish. And this is what happens when we detach and decode our map of meaning and then decide to change. We come to life, the ordering begins, life changes for the good. A tree is a viable life form. Now she is upright. Now she cultivates parts that have functions. The roots can ground her. The trunk can move her higher in the hierarchy.

Compare that dream to one she reported in the first session, before she received the feedback. She said that the following was a recurring dream [1]that she has had from early childhood to the age of 27, every year or so, sometimes more frequently:

> A bright, white, soft glow that fills the whole space in front of me and my mind slowly fades to the image of a comic page that's been crumpled up, soaked in dirty water and then pressed flat again so the creases are darkened and pronounced. On the comic pages the scene of a man wearing tattered clothes and torn gloves and a wool hat, crouched in on himself, standing behind a dumpster in an alley smoking as rain beats down.

Could the light represent divinity/order which enters a life space characterized by deficiency and chaos? The down and out character, a product of a worn, tired map of meaning; a comic page because it is the narrative of a child, a worn document that is now rightly a discard, one step from the dumpster where it belongs. A man in a state of chaos. No order to be found. Not yet. But since we all move from chaos to order, the dream implies potential. There is, after all, light near at hand.

Karen has been coming of age. Accessing the map of meaning was the first step that catapulted more forward motion. allowing her to make dramatic changes and so upgrade and revise the map of her youth. Karen is on her way. That map is changing! The early memories helped her find her way.

Notes

1. It is thought that recurrent dreams indicate the presence of unresolved conflicts or otherwise indicate the experience of ongoing stressors. Research indicates that recurrent dreams tend to orient around negative dream content and have been correlated with diminished experience of psychological well-being (Zadra, 1996).

12

Understanding the Messenger and the Message

The greatest happiness is simply knowing one's direction. Even if one has not yet started along the road; simply knowing which road to follow in life is a great elation.

Rabbi Akiva Tatz

I hope this book comes full circle. We have explored Peterson's map of meaning, and explored how that map manifests by looking at early memories. Now I want to wrap up with some thoughts on Peterson, the man.

I mentioned earlier that the Talmud teaches that little prophesy exists today, but one remaining form occurs when parents name their children; supposedly, a name describes essence. In other words, parents are granted inspiration so that they will choose a name for the child that captures the child's essence. In that spirit, let's consider the meaning of Peterson's first name. We need to consider who this man is, why we are riveted by him, why he possesses an eloquence that is clearly inspired. And why he also galvanizes a lot of resistance.

Hebrew words reveal their meaning when we analyze them; we will often find encoded within other words and letters. Jordan is a Hebrew name. In Hebrew, the word reads '*Yarden.*' Within that word we find the Hebrew word '*yored*', a verb that implies lowering something or something descending, and we find a Hebrew letter, *Nun.* The Jordan River is named as such because that river drops dramatically along its course. When we look at that Hebrew name '*Yarden*', we read, "*yored Nun*:" the lowering of '*Nun*'. But what is *Nun*?

You've heard of the Nuns, right? Women known for their piety. Every Hebrew letter represents a concept. The concept of *Nun* refers to spiritual transcendence, often that which occurs as a byproduct of adversity. Or as Peterson reflects, "we don't know what extreme experiences you need to go through to have extreme experiences [i.e. spiritual awakenings], but [those higher spiritual experiences] don't usually occur when you are eating cheesies and playing Mario Brothers!" Think *Nun*, think 'baptism by fire', the dark night of the soul that often leads someone to open spiritual channels and explore teachings from the wisdom traditions.

Additionally, each Hebrew letter associates with a number. *Nun* associates with the number 50. The *Zohar*, an ancient mystical text, is one of several sources which discusses "the 50 Gates of Understanding." Through extensive character development and via undergoing ordeals, the student reaches for this higher state of consciousness, associated with the number 50, which transports his or her understanding beyond the mundane to the heart of reality, itself.

Jordan is he who brings down knowledge leading to spiritual transcendence, knowledge which he has been able to access because he has navigated treacherous ordeals.

Jordan as Water

Another aspect of the word '*Yarden*' associates to water, as in the river that bears that name. What is water? One Torah commentator, the *Maharal*, describes water as the most perfect creation. *Rashi*, a prominent commentator, effectively points out that we never hear about the creation of water in the creation narrative. When water is mentioned in Genesis, line 2, it already exists. Water, he deduced, is created well before the time documented as the starting point of creation. It would appear that water, then, enjoys a special and unique status amongst all the creations.

And why shouldn't it? It is unique. Water is comprised of two different elements and the joining of both takes them to a new format, one with special import given its life giving properties and the fact that the human body is 80% water. Water is unique in that it assumes one of three different formats depending on temperature. Three, of course, is a meaningful number according to many traditions.

The spiritual traditions agree that water represents the archetype of the sage. In Deuteronomy 32:2, Moses exclaims: "My doctrine shall drop as the rain, My speech shall distil as the dew; As the small rain upon the tender grass, And as the showers upon the herb."

Tao Cheng, a Chinese sage, writes that water corresponds to the archetype of the Sage, citing the many paradoxical properties of that element: it yields, making its way around rocks and obstacles. Yet, it always prevails, finding its way to the sea. It corrodes hard metal and extinguishes fire but, if it will otherwise be defeated, it escapes as steam. One who models him or herself after water will be an exemplar of humility, following the modus operandi of that element. Such a person "embraces passivity, acts from nonaction and conquers the world." (as quoted in Beinfield & Korngold, 1991)

The name Jordan, then, implies much: the task of bringing down teachings, which, like water, emanate from above; teachings designed to transform and elevate the learner, those 'down' below. He's certainly doing that. And he who brings down *Nun*, undergoes severe personal ordeals, part of what prepares him to be the messenger of special wisdom.

Jordan's Dream

In *Maps of Meaning*, Peterson shares a powerful nightmare he had, which awakened him to his life task at a point when he was feeling stymied and confused. He turned to his dreams for guidance and initially received none. Then he woke with a dream within a dream.

The dream had him in a two-storey house that was apparently his. He had been drinking heavily and so went to the attic of this house where he fell asleep. From there he had the following dream, embedded within the original dream:

There was a huge chandelier hanging beneath the dome in a darkened cathedral. Peterson was trapped in that chandelier which hung hundreds of feet down from the ceiling, yet hundreds of feet above the ground floor. The people below him looked like ants, owing to his distance from them. Those people were in charge of the cathedral and opposed Peterson's station in the chandelier. They protested his presence in the chandelier. He, himself, was unhappy with this placement and wanted to leave.

At this point in the dream, Peterson shakes himself awake, but in so far as this is a dream within a dream, he is now awake in the dream but still actively dreaming. He woke himself as a means of escaping the chandelier, but, even once awake in the dream, finds he is still ensconced in the chandelier. He then tries to fall back asleep in the dream; if he is stuck up there he figures it's better to dream this circumstance then actually live it. He is not able to fall back asleep in the dream.

In the next part of the dream, he finds himself on the ground. He only wished to get back to his home so he could sleep. He arrived home. He's in a small windowless room, maybe a furnace room, on the ground floor. This room connected to others around it, but had no direct access to get outside the house. There was a single bed in the room. Now a "strange wind descended" [1]on him. "Under its influence, [he] started to dissolve." He is clear that this wind is going to take him right back to the chandelier in the center of the cathedral. He tried to fight the wind and fell into a convulsion. He tried to yell for help. Then he awoke to discover the window behind his bed was wide open and the wind was blowing into the room. He stumbled out of bed, closed the window but the terror stayed with him for some time. (Peterson, 1999, p. 460).

"*Yored Nun*"

Let's look at this dream to see the calling of he whose job is to "*yored Nun.*" Allow me to reprint the second line of Genesis here:

"when the earth was astonishingly empty, with darkness upon the surface of the deep, and the Divine Presence hovered upon the surface of the waters"

As described in an earlier chapter, we understand from this line the constituent parts of creation in the lower domain: chaos, rife full of potential, on the ground level; the Divine Presence hovering above it. He whose job is to bring down the spiritual teachings finds himself forced – by destiny itself – to be uncomfortably ensconced in the upper domain, the chandelier of the cathedral. It would make sense that the chandelier houses those spiritual teachings which promote enlightenment. The task is uncomfortable. The physical body is not majestically hosted in the upper realm, which governs all that is ethereal, like light. The body prefers the earth.

This dream is reminiscent of the account in the Torah when Moses is summonsed to perform a duty, to lead the Jewish people to freedom and to counter Pharoah, their oppressor. Moses tries to talk his way out of that job.

And who wouldn't want to wiggle out of this type of calling. There will be multiple ordeals associated with this job. The angry mob below represent the chaos of the human condition below; those at a far distance from the Divine Presence will fight and resist its message; living in the physical substrate, so far from those teachings which could help order their lives and subdue their chaotic emotions, those below look like ants. Why? With limited access to higher teachings, they exist in a contracted state. They are small.

Now *Nun* energy, as mentioned above, when manifested in the less progressive way, takes the form of inebriation or sleep, both states which take a person out of the mundane world of physicality and elevates them, potentially for the better good . . . or not. Mystical sources teach that when asleep the soul ascends to the upper worlds. The least intimidating and least effortful way of doing *Nun* is by sleeping or using alcohol or drugs. And while the dreaming Jordan prefers to sleep, looks to reclaim his bed and get back to sleep, he is thrust back, again and again, to reclaim his uncomfortable position in the chandelier; wakefulness interrupts sleep, and when he finally lands he is overtaken by the wind, be it the windy weather conditions or convulsions, representing an inner wind.

Wind symbolizes the movement that must prevail on the earth. The Hebrew word for earth, "*Aretz*," has "*Rutz*" or 'running' embedded within it. The earth associates with frenetic movement. The wind also relates to the breath of the Divine, a force that seems intent to send him back to the chandelier. And the room is surrounded by other rooms and cut off from the outside, indicating, I suspect, that the physical world is characterized by fragmentation. The unity perspective associated with the Divine, the perspective one gets when looking at a scene from a higher vantage point, is not easily accessed when in the lower domain..

So there on the ground floor, Peterson cannot sleep. He has to move. And the space in the basement is isolating, separate, connoting the emptiness we read about in Genesis, line 2. His next step is clear. He cannot ignore the state of chaos on the ground level. He has to assume the uncomfortable position of moving into the public eye, facing criticism and resistance from the mob, and channeling the wisdom tradition, aka getting back into that damn chandelier.

Destiny calls. It's not going to be comfortable. A lesser man would go back to sleep and leave it at that but if this man avoids his calling, he will be tormented by the chaos down below anyway; he certainly won't get the sleep he craves, so he might as well get to work. Peterson understands that a life of spiritual depth comes with a price tag.

Peterson reports that as a young man he abused drugs and alcohol. But in the dream, when he shakes himself out of the alcohol-induced sleep, he rejects sleep or alcohol, the more indulgent way of doing *Nun*, taking on the task of naming the chaos in the lower creation (which he effectively does by recounting the dream). Reclaiming his position in the chandelier means he will wield the knowledge and teachings that he accesses by reaching into the higher dimension. He will '*yored Nun*', doing the job that is his, heeding the task that crystalized when he was named. When he wakes from the dream in real life, he understands the dream and his mission, remembering John 14:12: "... He that believes in me, the works that I do shall he do also and greater works than these shall he do..." His task is huge. His burden, large. He will bear it.

Life as a Dream within a Dream

What of the dream within the dream? Some traditions teach that the physical reality which feels like 'reality' is only a mask for the true reality: a physical world that has a hidden, but very real spiritual infrastructure (Tatz, 1995). We live in a world rife with chaos which we can organize if we access the wisdom of the Divine Presence and execute Its inspired vision. We, too, can assume a position in the chandelier, can fight off the urge to sleep through the higher calling. These dynamics sit at the core of reality, so when we ultimately awaken to this true reality, it will be like waking from a dream. Our current day-to day-lives, which feel so real, will be revealed as a facade. We were dreaming, all along. Then, finally, we will be awake.

Back to Peterson

Peterson shares a great wealth of ideas and information in his books and talks. Many of his articulations are lucid and insightful. Some, though, have not hit the mark for me. For example, he shared some interesting concepts in his talks on Genesis but clearly did not access important ideas, work of some of the most prolific and respected commentators. Some of those classic texts provide rich support for the very insights he promotes. His work would have been greatly enriched with their inclusion. Other times, for lack of access to arguably the most venerated and authoritative commentaries, he advanced interpretations which were, according to my understanding, off the mark. Despite my areas of disagreement, what excites me about his work is that he often represents some aspect of reality or psychology so accurately – seemingly seeing reality through a clear lens and expressing what he comprehends so eloquently that we get an 'aha' moment.

Peterson is teaching something about the contours of reality. Read the comments below each YouTube lecture. You read that people are finding his teachings helps them live better. Maybe they have better flow? Less false starts? More success? Something is helping these people.

And Finally

I had to do this book. Remember how names capture essence? I am Annette . . . read 'a net.'

Peterson, in one lecture, refers to a myth wherein the protagonist encapsulates chaos, putting it into a net. Peterson interpreted the net as symbolizing the way something large and complex can be contained conceptually. We can use an overarching conceptual structure – symbolized by the net – to get a handle on chaos, something not so easy to get a handle on.

That idea spoke to me! I am 'a net'! My motive is to cluster useful ideas and create overarching conceptual structures, meta-maps which help me understand reality. As Peterson's work attests, creating conceptual structures provides a reference that people can use to interpret reality, make better decisions and act more effectively. In that spirit, my intent, true to my name, has been to give readers an overarching view of some of the ideas of Peterson and Adler. If there is more work to do, in terms of cracking open your own memories and discerning what they are telling you, you may consult the Adlerian books I mention in Chapter 8 or consult a book I list in the Recommended Reading section that will take your interpretation skills to the next level. Or you can reach out to an Adlerian therapist if you wish to garner more information/interpretation of your 10 earliest memories.

May this book, a work in progress and the first of a series, represent some of Peterson's ideas so as to help you move your goals forward. And may this summary, Peterson's work, and the writings of Adler and other interesting thinkers continue to help you (and I'll quote Peterson here) "to design your personality in a manner that would have you thrilled to be alive!"

Notes

1. In the Hebrew Bible, there are countless mentions of the prohibition: "Don't worship strange gods." One scholar, Rabbi Wolpe teaches that we should interpret that phrase not as 'strange gods' but as the forces of estrangement, those forces that create disharmony and conflict. They detract from our experience of comraderie. In Peterson's dream, I see the strange wind as the forces that promote estrangement between people, tribes, etc. Peterson, himself, has been a target of such forces.

13

Epilogue: The Nutshell

Milton H. Erickson, MD, was a gifted and prolific psychiatrist, the father of modern day hypnosis. His techniques were legendary and often defied comprehension. A creative genius, there are many compilations of his most interesting and zany interventions which helped clients achieve dramatic change. Readers are encouraged to read Jay Haley's *Uncommon Therapy: The Psychiatric Techniques of Milton H. Erickson* to get an orientation to this masterful work.

Erickson attracted a cadre of students, entry-level psychotherapists who were eager to learn his methods. His followers tried to simplify his methods and many published books. Amongst them were Richard Bandler and John Grinder who published a two-volume set, *Patterns of the Hypnotic Technique of Milton H. Erickson, Volumes 1 & 2*. They claimed to have captured the language patterns that Erickson was using to help his clients achieve deep hypnotic trance. After they published their set, Erickson made the following wry comment: "Bandler and Grinder think they've got the whole thing in a nutshell. Little do they know, they only have the nutshell!"

In my modest effort to come up with a partial summary of the first two chapters of Jordan Peterson's *Maps of Meaning: The Architecture of Belief*, I am dwarfed by the task. So here's my epilogue: I get it. This is just the nutshell!!

My hope is that with some of his premises spelled out, you might now be able to crack into his book and get more out of it. You should find it easier to follow the thread when you are listening to his talks or online courses, now that you have certain ideas under your belt, so to speak.

As a next step, I want to encourage you to continue the learning, reading, listening. To do that you might engage with the many Jordan Peterson Facebook discussion groups that contemplate Peterson's ideas. There is a wonderful community of people from around the world who are processing Peterson's ideas and discussing how they are implementing them to make their lives better.

In short: You are not done! This was the beginning! If I've been successful, you will have better traction as you move forward in these studies. I pray that my efforts have helped you. I look forward to continuing to learn alongside you. May Dr. Peterson and his family be blessed with good health and vitality, allowing him to share his wisdom with us for many, many years into the future.

Annette Poizner, MSW, Ed.D, RSW

Toronto, Canada

Recommended Reading

I'd like to recommend some follow-up reading. If you haven't already, I strongly encourage you to pick up a copy of Peterson's books which need no introduction:

Maps of Meaning: The Architecture of Belief by Jordan Peterson

12 Rules for Life: An Antidote to Chaos by Jordan Peterson

And other relevant works:

Strangers to Ourselves: Discovering the Adaptive Unconscious by Timothy Wilson

To further unpack the faculty that governs the implicit non-declarative memory, also known as the unconscious, read Timothy Wilson and learn what we know about the unconscious mind based on scientific study. This is the best book that gives you a living and breathing clarity about the part of the mind that we are referring to when we speak about the unconscious, that part of the mind that harbours your map of meaning.

How the World Sees You by Sally Hogshead

This book outlines a personality system that I find quite intriguing. It's worth visiting her site to take her questionnaire, and looking at the book to clarify more about your type, or others you know. Type speaks strongly to the map of meaning unique to each person.

Dawn of Memories: The Meaning of Early Recollections in Life by Arthur J Clarke

Need more information and insight to figure out the meaning of your 10 memories? Read this book for a more in depth treatment on this subject.

Godless: The Church of Liberalism by Ann Coulter
Oprah: The Gospel of an Icon by Kathryn Lofton

Read really interesting analyses of pseudo-religions that seem to have replaced more traditional religions.

The Path: What Chinese Philosophers Can Tell Us about Living the Good Life by Michael Puett and Christine Gross-Loh

Eastern philosophy provides rich insights that can help us move away from rigidities that may be promoted in outdated maps from yesteryear. This is a very accessible book. I suspect Peterson would like many of the ideas therein which are effectively describing the chaos that underpins reality.

100 Names for Love: A Memoir by Diane Ackerman

The Honey Bus: A Memoir of Loss, Courage and a Girl Saved by Bees by Meredith May

The Prize Winner of Defiance, Ohio: How My Mother Raised 10 Children on 25 Words or Less by Terry Ryan

It can be quite inspiring to read biographies and autobiographies about people and their struggle to move from chaos to order. I strongly recommend the above three books.

Uncommon Therapy: The Psychiatric Techniques of Milton H Erickson, MD by Jay Haley

Strongly recommended. Classic psychotherapists have historically tried to bring order to chaos, higher reasoning to emotional intensities from yesteryear. The great Milton Erickson brought chaos to order, understanding the people have habitually used their symptoms to create a type of order in their lives that needs to be disrupted. This work is fabulously creative, insightful, inspiring and often downright hysterical. A must-read.

Additional Resources

Dr. Jordan B. Peterson's website

Dr. Peterson's personality assessment profile for individuals

http://www.understandyourself.com

Dr. Peterson's Self-authoring Suite

http://www.selfauthoring.com

Bibliography

Beinfield, Harriet & Korngold, Efrem (1991). *Between Heaven and Earth: A Guide to Chinese Medicine*. New York: Ballantine Books.

Bennetts, Leslie (2016). *Last Girl Before the Freeway: The Life, Loves, Losses and Liberation of Joan Rivers*. New York: Little, Brown and Company

Brooks, David (2019). *The Second Mountain: The Quest for a Moral Life*. New York City: Random House Publishers.

Coulter, Ann (2006). *Godless: The Church of Liberalism*. Crown Publishers.

Fisher, Carrie (2011). *Shockaholic*. New York: Simon & Shuster.

Fisher, Carrie (2016). *The Princess Diarist*. New York: Blue Rider Press.

Hillman, James & Ventura, Michael (1992). *We've Had a Hundred Years of Psychotherapy and the World is Getting Worse*. San Francisco: HarperCollins Publishers.

Kurtz, Ron & Prestera, Hector (1979). *The Body Reveals: An Illustrated Guide to the Psychology of the Body*. New York: Harper & Row.

Lofton, Kathryn (2011). *Oprah: The Gospel of an Icon*. Oakland, CA: University of California Press

Peck, M.S. (1978). *The Road Less Traveled: A New Psychology of Love, Traditional Values and Spiritual Growth*. New York: Simon & Shuster

Peterson, Jordan (1999). *Maps of Meaning: The Architecture of Belief*. New York: Routledge

Peterson, Jordan (2017). *12 Rules for Life: An Antidote to Chaos*. New York: Penguin Random House

Peterson, Jordan. Lectures:

"The Psychological Significance of the Bible," 17 videos

"Personality and its Transformation," 2017, 20 videos

"Maps of Meaning: The Architecture of Belief," 2017, 12 videos

"Maps of Meaning" TVO series

Additional extraneous Peterson YouTube videos.

Poizner, Annette (2003). Graphology in psychotherapy: A Pilot Study exploring clients' and psychotherapists' perceptions of graphology use. Unpublished dissertation.

Poizner, Annette (2011). Symbolism in Handwriting. *Semiotica*, 185 (1/4), 113-122

Poizner, Annette (2102). *Clinical Graphology: An Interpretive Manual for Mental Health Practitioners*. Springfield, Illinois: Charles C Thomas Publisher.

Poizner, Annette (2019). *An Illustrated Guide to Using Jordan Peterson's Insights Regarding Divinity & the Map of Meaning*. Toronto: Lobster University Press

Poizner, Annette (2019). *Clean Your Room: An Out-of-the-Box Manual for Lobsters*. Toronto: Lobster University Press

Poizner, Annette (2020). *In Good Standing: Using Jordan Peterson's Insights into the Structure of Self to Sort Yourself Out*. Toronto: Lobster University Press

Poizner, Annette (2019). This Way Up: A Faith-Based Introduction to Jordan Peterson's 'Maps of Meaning'. Toronto: Lobster University Press

Powers, Robert & Griffith, Jane (1987). *Understanding Life-Style: The Psycho Clarity Process.* Adlerian Psychology Associates, Ltd.

Puett, Michael and Gross-Loh, Christine (2016). *The Path: What Chinese Philosophers Can Teach Us about Living the Good Life*. New York: Simon & Shuster

Rivers, Joan (1986). *Enter Talking*. New York: Dell Publishing Company.

Rohr, Richard (2010). *Falling Upward: A Spirituality for the Two Halves of Life*. Accessible Publishing Systems.

Rovelli, Carlo (2017). *The Order of Time.* Maine: Thorndike.

Shulman, Bernard & Mosak, Harold (1988) *Manual for Life Style Assessment.* Muncie, Indiana: Accelerated Development, Inc.

Stone Edition (2001). *The Chumash.* Brooklyn, New York: Mesorah Publications.

Tatz, Akiva (1993). *Living Inspired.* Southfield, Michigan: Targum Press.

Tatz, Akiva (1995). *Worldmask.* Southfield, Michigan: Targum Press.

Zadra, A. (1996). Recurrent dreams: Their relation to life events. In D. Barrett (ed.). *Trauma and Dreams.* Cambridge: MA. Harvard University Press.

14

Acknowledgements

In the last decades, many bestselling works have influenced the thinking of a generation. Yet, Jordan Peterson's work is unique. He has triggered dialogue worldwide – not among clinicians and academics (who seem to dismiss him) but amongst the population at large. Groups and get-togethers are organized in cities around the world to discuss and advance his ideas about life and its meaning. Online discussion groups bring together Peterson devotees from around the world to analyze and discuss his work.

This book is a product of that ongoing conversation. I am grateful to various members of these online groups who have shared thoughts, read this work, offered critiques and comments and otherwise encouraged and shaped this project. One reader, a wise soul in India, participated extensively to honour the memory of Mr. David Sassoon, a Jewish benefactor who built hospitals and schools in India 200 years ago; to this day millions have benefited owing to his generosity. I am grateful for R's wisdom and likewise honour the memory of Mr. David Sassoon, z'l. I'm also indebted to D.Y.P. for her many improvements and for her wise insights based on her own life experience. The idea of questions for readers to ponder was hers. About these reflection points, she mused, "maybe Peterson would say that that is putting responsibility on the reader to imbibe the message and that's a bloody good thing!" I thought every idea she contributed was spot on!

Of course, I must express my gratitude to Dr. Jordan B. Peterson for his tireless efforts to discuss and share important ideas and for generously making his work available to a wide audience.

And finally, may I thank my Creator, who I otherwise refer to in this volume as G-d (in deference to a Jewish tradition which avoids the full elaboration of a name that expresses Divinity). May the ideas expressed within this work help me – and others – to find Divinity in the shadows while enduring those ordeals which are a necessary part of the hero's journey.

About the Author

Annette Poizner, MSW, Ed.D., RSW

Annette Poizner is a Toronto-based therapist in private practice who functions as a life coach and executive coach when working with clients around the world. She completed her Masters degree in Social Work at Columbia University of New York and a Doctorate in Education (specializing in Counseling Psychology) at the University of Toronto. In her practice of the last 28 years, she routinely performs projective personality assessment in the context of psychotherapy and within a life coaching practice which has her working with individuals around the world via phone or video.

Projective personality assessment has clinicians deciphering the client's map of meaning by analyzing dreams, memories, handwriting samples and other materials clients submit for this purpose. She has specialized training in techniques developed by Dr. Milton Erickson, as well as advanced training in the use of Eye Movement Desensitization Reprocessing (EMDR) and Neuro Linguistic Programming (NLP). She is the co-founder of the Milton H. Erickson Institute of Toronto.

Her work had been featured in dailies across Canada, in trade magazines across North America, and in clinical and academic venues such as at the Canadian Psychological Association annual conference and other professional meetings. Her blog on the Huffington Post discussed all matters pertaining to handwriting. She is the author of a textbook published by a leading scholarly publishing house. "*Clinical Graphology: An Interpretive Manual for Mental Health Practitioners.*" To date she has published six volumes under the Lobster University Press imprint: A *Practical Summary & Workbook for Using Jordan Peterson's Maps of Meaning to Sort Yourself Out, An Illustrated Guide to Using Jordan Peterson's Insights Regarding Divinity and the Map of Meaning to Sort Yourself Out, In Good Standing: Using Jordan Peterson's Insights on the Structure of Self to Sort Yourself Out, This Way Up: A Faith-Based Introduction to Jordan Peterson's Maps of Meaning , Clean Your Room: An Out-of-the-Box Manual for Lobsters* and *From Chaos to Order: A Guide to Jordan Peterson's Worldview. Beyond Chaos: Wrestling with Jordan Peterson's Insights on the Feminine.* An upcoming volume, *Yin, Yang & You: An Eastern Commentary on Jordan Peterson's 12 Rules for Life* is due out in the Fall, 2020.

You can read more about her work on her blog on the Times of Israel and her blog on Medium.com. She has also makes very short animation videos, intent to communicate soundbites of Peterson's teachings 'in a New York minute'. You can subscribe to the Lobster University Press YouTube channel. You can access many of her other publications on her website, ap.annettepoizner.com. To be advised of the release of the next book in this series or to contact her with feedback about this work (which will be sporadically updated) please email ap@annettepoizner.com or follow the Facebook page, where she will publish ideas, updates and revisions.

Lobster University Press

Jordan Peterson's *Maps of Meaning: The Architecture of Belief* and the opus of his work, more generally, is vast in scope and complex in nature. I have launched Lobster University Press, named tongue in cheek, for sure, but also with a vision in mind. Peterson relays many ideas that we can unpack, ideas that can help us scale the hierarchy or get a tougher shell to endure life's hardships; maybe even indirectly raise the production of serotonin! The books I publish will focus on specific themes addressed by Peterson in his books and lectures to help readers better integrate the material, expand their 'map of meaning' and tweak that most important of abilities: the capacity to "turn chaos into habitable order!" These works will be the product of discourse and exchange with other Peterson enthusiasts, as we all continue to mine the depth of Peterson's work and explore interesting and helpful applications.

Explore Volume 2 of this series:

An Illustrated Guide for Using Jordan Peterson's Insights on Divinity & the Map of Meaning to Sort Yourself Out

By Annette Poizner, MSW, Ed.D., RSW

According to Dr. Jordan Peterson, secular society has overlooked the psychological importance of Divinity, failing to understand the template it provides that helps us flourish. If Peterson is right, we need to review what classic texts tell us about the intricate and specific structure of the G-dhead. Lo and behold, that exact structure pervades creation as a whole, serving as DNA that undergirds the physical world, the human body, the contours of the psyche and more.

In this book, Psychotherapist Annette Poizner first explores Peterson's insights about Divinity, then traces the imprint of Divinity on creation. Exploring the nooks and crannies of our world – surveying diverse areas including graphic design, cultural norms, marketing practices, handedness and more – allows us to see unity, the watermark of Divinity, at the root of creation. As we explore the central pattern at play, we delve into a visual adventure: learning the structure of Divinity by – believe it or not – analyzing the handwriting of public figures.

Poizner introduces Clinical Graphology, a bona fide European technique for assessing personality, to illustrate how the template of Divinity is our first and only nature. Learning about Oprah, Streisand, Deepak Chopra and others, you will learn about yourself! Explore the profound truths about self and soul that flow each time you pick up a pen . . . en route to our ultimate destination, not to know the rich and famous, but to know G-d and Self. As Poizner writes, "If the Divine infrastructure is intrinsically relevant to us, then societal disinterest and abandonment of the G-d ideal not only banishes G-d but, in some sense, ourselves. We may not know who, or how, to be." Of course, this is exactly Peterson's point.

In a work 15 years in the making, Poizner weaves together the ideas of Jordan Peterson, Jewish Mysticism, Chinese medical theory, Jungian psychology, and 30 years of clinical experience, to survey the interior of our world from a most unique vantage point.

Explore Volume 3 of this series:

This Way Up: A Faith-Based Introduction to Jordan Peterson's 'Maps of Meaning'

By Annette Poizner, MSW, Ed.D., RSW

Jordan Peterson's books are selling furiously, widely cited in the media and part of an ongoing conversation. This book addresses why those in the faith-based communities should familiarize themselves with this work. Psychotherapist Annette Poizner argues that Peterson's work is awakening the hearts and minds of a generation, prompting an army of young people to question the premises of secularism and ponder the tenets of faith. In this *zeitgeist*, clergy and laypeople are better equipped to address the needs of young people walking through their doors if they understand the worldview Peterson is advancing. This book is designed to summarize some of Peterson's important concepts including his ideas about the nature of reality and its constituent aspects, the structure of the mind, and the psychological necessity of the G-d ideal. These ideas will be presented through the lens of faith, referring to teachings which are drawn from a detailed study of the text of Genesis, so believers of monotheistic religions can explore how Peterson's concepts can be personally useful to readers of various faiths and denominations.

Explore Volume 4 of this series:

Clean Your Room: An Out-of-the-Box Manual for Lobsters

By Annette Poizner, MSW, Ed.D., RSW

The presidential nominations are underway & Dr. Jordan Peterson nominates you . . . to take bold steps to move your life forward. Ready to turn a new leaf in 2020? Peterson Super Fan Annette Poizner, a therapist, educator and author, extends Peterson's maxim 'Clean your room', making the case for lifestyle changes that may not be on your radar. Contemplating the start of a new decade, Poizner takes instruction from the first beginning on record, as it is conceived in Genesis. Can lessons embedded in that narrative speak to the contemporary lifestyle? Poizner makes the case that old wisdom, peppered with insights from Jordan Peterson, himself, will guide you toward better outcomes. Plan your New Year's Resolutions with the help of a seasoned therapist. Bring your 2020 vision into focus.

Explore Volume 5 of this series:

In Good Standing: Using Jordan Peterson's Insights on the Structure of Self to Sort Yourself Out

By Annette Poizner, MSW, Ed.D., RSW

Your self has a structure, indirectly alluded to by Dr. Jordan Peterson each time he counsels you to live in alignment, whenever he urges you to stand with your shoulders back and every time he urges you to notice where you're aiming. Even the English 'Personal Pronoun I' alludes to that structure. Look carefully. Back 8 words. See it? It's a straight line.

Therapist Annette Poizner asserts that the archetype of the line, unpacked, delivers a myriad of lessons which can be applied to master the living of life. She will introduce the three-step pattern that underpins reality, expressed in hormonal patterns and stoplights, revealed in classic myths and modern-day acronyms, applied in building structures and hair braiding techniques. In all these, we find a trinity that sits at the root of creation, one referred to in the day-to-day vernacular as "beginning, middle and end," so naming the three points on a straight line. Watch as the contours of reality come into focus, bringing an awareness of a structure that pervades creation . . . and, more importantly, *yourself.*

Poizner, a seasoned clinician, doctoral level practitioner and certified graphologist, will pepper this presentation with references from the Hebrew Bible, other sources *and* with handwritings of prominent public figures! Turns out that we dance with the straight line each time we pick up a pen! We will meet the line in all its manifestations and befriend the archetype that grows us up, helps us stand tall, aims us forward and culminates, ideally, in a singular ego identity. We will come to see that each lie is nothing but a line with a missing piece and will understand that we spell our best success when we embrace the G-d-given archetype and, in so doing, actualize our Divine birthright. We have, after all, been lovingly made in the image of the One, the Only.

With a book designed to change your map of meaning and your perspective of life, you can take Peterson's ideas to the next level. Insights advanced by Rabbi Dr. Akiva Tatz, a Talmudic sage whose scope and intellect matches that of Peterson, will be harnessed by your guide, an author whose psychotherapy practice of 30 years compels a practical vision of what readers need to know to make meaningful and lasting life changes.

Explore Volume 6 of this series:

From Chaos to Order: A Guide to Jordan Peterson's Worldview

By Annette Poizner, MSW, Ed.D., RSW

Struggling to decipher Jordan Peterson's core worldview when you listen on YouTube? Finding that his mosaic style, fascinating tangents and detours into the mythic realm make him hard to follow? Or maybe you're wondering what the fuss is about and would like a concise introduction to Jordan Peterson's mentality, particularly as it relates to the task of sorting yourself out?

In this book, a seasoned therapist takes you on a tour of Peterson's central ideas. In a clear, linear presentation, Annette Poizner presents Peterson's premises about reality and the specific ways we perceive and organize that reality. She introduces his ideas regarding the map of meaning, outlines his take on how and why our life maps are easily corrupted and follows with his premises about the psychological necessity of the G-d ideal, tracing the sequelae when that ideal is absent, as it is in secular society. Finally, Poizner renders Peterson's map of the life space. We come to see how his rules help readers thrive in reality, given the contours of reality that he discusses. Prepare to see life from a unique, surprising and relevant vantage point.

In providing the scaffolding of Peterson's core arguments, Poizner gifts readers with a big picture that will help them when they read or listen to Peterson, facilitating better comprehension and alleviating some of the inevitable review normally required when working through his material. At the same time, this work bridges material from his two bestselling books, his Biblical lecture series and his

University of Toronto courses, depicting overarching themes that emerge across platforms and presenting those clinical insights that have implications for contemporary life. Readers gain a lens through which they can consider their own personal process and are given reflection points that they can use to explore the personal relevance of ideas discussed.

Please note: Four chapters from this practical summary have been reprinted in Volume 6.

Explore Volume 7 of this series:

Yin, Yang & You: An Eastern Commentary on Jordan Peterson's 12 Rules for Life

By Annette Poizner, MSW, Ed.D., RSW

Books that achieve bestseller status are often those that render essential truths, ideas core to our humanity. This is the case, says therapist Annette Poizner, regarding the works of Canadian psychologist Jordan Peterson. In this book, Poizner will analyze Peterson's *12 Rules for Life*, peering through the lens of Traditional Chinese Medicine's Five Element Theory in order to show how his material resonates deeply with a classic and ancient philosophical system.

Five Element Theory posits that five root elements underpin our world, our bodies and even our unique and varied psychologies. The theory renders a detailed understanding of how these elements are best choreographed to achieve a working harmony. Each element governs particular bodily systems but also relates to central psychological attributes. In *Yin, Yang & You*, we will see how Eastern truths shine out of Peterson's teachings, demonstrating why readers best heed Peterson's principles. Learn the infrastructure of your best self and clarify the choreography you can use to achieve it.

In creative chapters ('Learning How to Wok') that take readers on a tour through Peterson's worldview and Eastern premises of health, readers will learn the component parts of their psycho-spiritual constitutions and may come to recognize one particular element that constitutes their unique and personal soul root. Readers will garner lifestyle advice that will help them in their quest to balance the inner elements. We will explore 12 as the number that represents the harmonic integration of the masculine polarity, Yang (associated with the number one) with the feminine polarity, Yin (associated with the number two). In concluding chapters, we will look at the current state of the world, the impact of the Corona virus which has painfully corrected an overriding worldwide Yang excess/imbalance, counterbalancing it with a heavy-handed Yin redress. We will use ancient Chinese wisdom to help us chart a course, as we pursue the long-lost balance. Use Peterson's wisdom in tandem with ancient Eastern principles to find your way forward in the troubling and difficult times ahead.

Due out in September, 2020.
Volume 8 in this series:

Beyond Chaos: Wrestling with Jordan Peterson's Notion of the Feminine

By Annette Poizner, MSW, Ed.D., RSW

Thousands report that Jordan Peterson's insights have helped them achieve life-altering change. Yet, by Peterson's own admission, the lion's share of his followers are male. Are there jewels in his opus which could be accessed by women? Psychotherapist Annette Poizner says there are, but first this group needs to better understand what Peterson is actually saying about the feminine. Materials needs to be prepared which will speak to the female sensibility and help dismantle the resistance that prevents some women from approaching Peterson's work.

Does Peterson's talk of 'chaos' as feminine trigger you? Do you disagree with many of his political positions? Poizner asserts that approaching his material with a will to understand yields rewards: readers can benefit from insights, ideas that usefully deviate from the usual societal narrative, while maintaining the license to reject those (political or otherwise) that don't jibe for any given woman. She asserts that women *can* benefit from the materials that Peterson has generously shared online, leveraging insights to achieve significant personal change and delving into constructs of masculine and feminine that are as old as antiquity.

Annette Poizner, a writer, therapist and executive coach, brings unique credentials to the task of introducing Peterson's opus specifically to those women who have, to date, stood in opposition. Born in the 60's, Poizner grew up an avid feminist and remains committed to progress for women. Her clinical work, steeped in Chinese medical theory, the wisdom of the ancient Kabbalah and the psychology of Carl Jung, equips her to perform a rich and detailed rendering of *Yin* and *Yang*, masculine and feminine, towards the end of unpacking Peterson's frame in a way that brings the teachings to life.

Poizner, who herself differs with Peterson on a range of issues, is working to provide a bridge for women who need help getting over the hump: helping them understand where Peterson has been vilified and misquoted, where he advances clinical insight that can be used to make life better and where they can easily agree to disagree with him. In terms of the latter, in so doing women can deliciously host the paradox of life, itself; the paradox that the masculine and feminine polarities are, more than anything else, here to teach us; the paradox, that, more than anything else, represents the central task of life, what we are here to learn.

Made in the USA
Coppell, TX
25 November 2020

42099432R00115